Last Judgment
Posthumous

Last Judgment Posthumous

by Emanuel Swedenborg
Translated by John Whitehead

THE ENGLISH. The English appear a little to the right, in front, in a plane just above the head. The light with them appears more interior than with others in the Christian world, by which light the spiritual is received which flows in from above. They see clearly in a moment what flows in, and at once receive it; nor do they let it down into their natural so grossly as others. Hence it is that the spiritual appears clear also in the natural; but with others more obscure. But they who are such, are those who have loved what is right and sincere, and have acted from truth and sincerity, and who at the same time have thought of God from religion.

When the Last Judgment was being executed, the Protestants were then led into the middle, and they then appeared in this order: The English in the middle, the Dutch towards the east and south, the Germans more towards the north, the Swedes to the north and west in the middle. All then appeared according to their general genius as to the reception of good and truth.

Few of the English become genii, whose quality may be described, since they do not depend much on their own thought, but on the mouth of authority: for they easily receive if only they are persuaded that the man is learned and sincere, and of their own nation; their thought then appears lucid and interior.

It was perceived that many of the English will receive the Heavenly Doctrine, and thereby come into the New Jerusalem; because they are such that they receive the truths of faith more easily than others, and see them in interior light.

I have spoken with the English concerning their natural disposition; whence it is with them, that when they hear truths from one among them worthy of belief, they then see them, and thus easily conform to them; and whence it is that with them there is a snowy appearance above their natural, that it is from heavenly light, from which is intelligence: in like manner with the Dutch. But as to the Dutch, with them there is not that snowy appearance, but something firm in the confines of their spiritual and natural minds; and that therefore they are slower. The cause of the appearance of the light with the English was told, namely, that it is from their life, which differs from the life of all other nations. That the cause might be perceived, a comparison was made with the Italians of this day; that their governments are altogether opposite. In England there is freedom to speak and write both on civil and spiritual things; but no freedom at all to use deceit and cunning to deceive others, nor to lie in wait to murder, rob and kill; and if they do it, there is no remission. But it is the opposite with the Italians at this day. In Italy there is freedom to deceive by cunning and guile, and also to kill; which freedom they have from so many asylums, and from the dispensations: but there is no freedom at all to speak and write on ecclesiastical and civil affairs there, on account of the inquisition. Hence it is that the Italian nation retains such things within, and thus a fire, which is a slow hatred, revenge, and cruelty; which fire is like that which, after a conflagration, lies hid long under the ashes, and consumes. But with the English nation it is otherwise, because it is allowed to speak and write freely. There such a fire is not laid up, but immediately burns out; and they are kept in what is sincere and just by the fact that they are not permitted to deceive, to rob, and to kill; since there is then no dispensation, nor anywhere an asylum.

The English have quite an exquisite perception that a thing is so, when it is said from reason. They have an interior sight as to religion; but this sight which they have is a receptive sight, but not so active that they can see before it has been confirmed by some celebrated leader among them. Their interior sight is called the intuitive and affirmative sight of reception, and likewise confirmative; but chiefly by means of elegant things composed in a spiritual manner; and this descends and proceeds from that snowy appearance of theirs. This appears with them in the spiritual world; on which account also they are in the middle among Christians: for those are in the middle who are in interior light.

It was shown of what quality a book or writing appears to them, which has been approved by a man in whose erudition they have confidence; and of what quality a book or writing appears, which is not yet approved. In writings not approved, when they are read, they see nothing but the mere letter, or the sense of the letter; but in an approved writing they see the sense of the matter, and not of the letter; because they are then in enlightenment from the belief that it is so: so that approval gives enlightenment. On which account a writing, howsoever important, is not procured before it has been praised by a man worthy of belief.

Since the English are of such a genius, there are therefore set over them priests, and also magistrates, in whom they have confidence that they are intelligent and wise; and they then yield a favoring assent to them in everything which they say and teach. By this they are held in obedience, and likewise in doctrine. But they who are not compliant, and they who are wicked, are shut out of their society; for these loose the bond and unanimity.

I have had much discourse with English priests concerning faith, among whom also were bishops. Because it was according to their doctrine, they insisted that faith alone produces the endeavor to good. But to the question, whether by endeavor they meant man's manifest will, this they were unwilling to admit; because everything that proceeds from man's manifest will is in itself not good, and is meritorious; wherefore by endeavor they meant an internal operation, about which the understanding knows little: consequently that such endeavor is inwardly in faith, and that it is not manifested openly except by an inclination to doing. In this opinion they were so tenacious, and also in this, that faith produces the good which is called charity, that they were not willing to be led, although it was told them from heaven, that faith does not produce anything of charity, but that charity produces faith; and that faith before charity is not living faith, but only knowledge; and that a man ought to do good as of himself, and that otherwise nothing of good is inrooted and implanted: but to this they shut their ears. When they were told that one of the most talented of them 9-1 had thought out reasons and ways, even to a hundred, to confirm that faith produces charity, and that he had wandered through each way, as is done in the spiritual world by thinking that it is so; but still, when he came to the end of the way, he saw from enlightenment given him that he had been wandering, which he also as often confessed. Also when their solemn exhortation at the Holy Supper was read before them, wherein these things are said, 9-2... they thought, but were unwilling to say, that this is said for the laity, and that the doctrine is for the clergy: wherefore it was announced to them, that life according to the faith of the laity saves; but life according to the doctrine of the clergy condemns: since in the faith of the clergy there is no life, and in their life there is no faith; but there is in the faith and life of the laity.

In the spiritual world images and many other things can be formed from the ideas of thought, and be presented to the sight; which is peculiar to that world. Wherefore the same English priests undertook to form an image in the likeness of a man, from the ideas of their thoughts concerning faith alone, or faith separate from charity; which image, when it was made, appeared monstrous, as not unlike Dagon, the idol of the Philistines in Ekron; therefore it was cast into a certain lake.

It is said of the English in the spiritual world, that they love elegance in their discourses; and that such elegance has indeed a delightful sound in the ears, but still gives little instruction; especially when they treat of faith, and of justification by it: that they then so arrange their words, that scarcely anyone knows whether anything of good is to be done or not. They so weave together series of conclusions, that they sound as if good should be done; although these conclusions involve that faith produces them without their knowing it.

In the spiritual world the face of the earth is similar to what it is in the natural world. There are urban and country places there. They who dwelt in cities in our world, dwell also in cities there: in like manner those who lived in country places. Moreover, the cities in the spiritual world are similar to the cities in the natural world, but only as to the streets and public squares; but they are not similar as to the buildings. Neither do the good and the evil dwell promiscuously there; but in the middle of the city, where also are the public buildings, 12-1 dwell the best, who are the governors and magistrates. To the east there are those who are in the clear good of love, to the west those who are in the obscure good of love, to the south those who are in the clear light of truth, to the north those who are in the obscure light of truth. The good of love and the truth of faith decrease from the middle into the farthest circumferences. Since the cities there are similar to the cities in our world, there is also a London there similar to London as to the streets; but not as to the houses, neither as to the inhabitants, nor their habitations in the quarters. I was conducted into it in the spirit, and wandered through it, and recognized it. And I spoke with certain ones there, and said that men in the world would wonder, and would not believe that they who live in London see a London also after death; and if they are good, also dwell in their city: yet it is altogether so. They said that neither would they have believed it, when they were in the world; because such a thing does not fall into sensual ideas, but only into rational ideas enlightened by spiritual light; also that they did not then know that the spiritual appears before a spirit, as the material does before a man; and that all the things which exist in the spiritual world are from a spiritual origin, as all the things in the natural world are from a material origin: in like manner the houses of a city, which are not built as in the world, but rise up in a moment created by the Lord: so too all other things. They rejoiced that now as before they are in England, and in its great city; and they said that there is also another London below, not dissimilar as to the streets, but dissimilar as to the houses and as to the inhabitants: namely, that the evil dwell in the middle, and the upright in the last circumferences; and that those come into that London from the London in the world, who have not been in any spiritual love, and hence not in any spiritual faith, but have indulged the pleasures of the body and the lusts of the mind. Also that the city, in the middle where the evil dwell, sinks down by turns into the deep; and the evil are thus cast down into hell: and that the opening is renewed, and the evil are again collected into the middle of it, and again are swallowed up by hell. This is in the world of spirits, it is different in heaven, and different in hell.

THE DUTCH. They are quite clear-sighted, and remain constantly in their own religion; not receding unless altogether convinced; and if they are convinced, they still turn the back. They excel in judgment from natural rational light, from which they look into things in the world justly, especially in business. Their light appears more obscure, because their spiritual light is conjoined with natural light: the reason is, because they are continually thinking about business.

With the Dutch there is not that snowy appearance which is with the English, but in place of it something firm; which is an indication that they are constant in the things of their religion. But there is this difference, that on civil, moral, and likewise spiritual subjects, they judge from themselves, and not from others: and they reflect especially upon intellectual things, and upon the connection of reasons.

The Dutch appear in the angle towards the east and south; to the east because they love religion bare without images, that they may look at it in itself, but not from images; to the south, because they excel in understanding.

It is a general trait of the Dutch nation, that they are strong in judgment from natural light, from which they take a very just view of things, especially of those that are of the world: and because they are continually thinking about their business, the spiritual light hides itself in the natural; on which account also they are able to receive what is true in religion: but still, when they are convinced, they turn the back.

The Dutch are not so eager for money as for business itself. Business itself is their end and love, and is in the first place; and money is the mediate end, and is loved for the sake of business; thus it is in the second place. And they who are such, are loved in heaven; each one is esteemed according to his use. It is otherwise with the avaricious, as the Jews are, with whom money is in the first place as the very end and love, and business in the second place. Hence is avarice, which is sordid according to the love of money alone.

At the day of the Last Judgment, those of the Dutch who had done nothing of good from any religion or conscience, but only for the sake of reputation, that for the sake of gain they might appear sincere, were cast out of their cities, villages and lands: for with such, when the regard for reputation and gain is taken away, which is done in the spiritual world, then such rush into every wickedness, despoiling whomsoever they happen to meet in the fields or outside of the cities. I saw a great number of such cast into a dark chasm extending obliquely under the eastern tract, and likewise into a chasm extending under the southern tract. This expulsion was seen on the 9th day of January, 1757. Those remained with whom there was religion and from religion conscience.

I was in the spirit, and it was then granted me to wander through a rather distinguished city, in which were Dutch. All the streets in it were seen to be roofed over, and in the streets were closed gates of wood; on which account, without leave from some overseer, it was not permitted to wander around. But afterwards it was granted me to speak with the magistrates, who dwelt in the middle of the city; by whom I was examined as to whence I came, and what I wanted: and when they understood that it was only for the sake of seeing, that I might make known to their brethren who were still in the world, what their lot was, and what kind of dwellings they had; they then related to me many things, especially that they who dwelt there were among the prudent and intelligent from that nation; and that there are many such cities, distinct according to the affections and perceptions of truth from good; and that they were in the world of spirits; and that after some time passed there, they were taken up thence into heaven, and introduced into societies there, and became angels: also that the city was double and triple, or city under city; and when one descends by ladders, he comes into a new city, where those reside who are different as to affections. They said that their streets are everywhere roofed over, because sometimes from the rocks round about, which are somewhat higher, they are looked at by the evil who are skilled in the perversion of souls by means of ideas, and in inducing lusts that are not congruous; and that they know how to bind the ideas, if by any means they penetrate; by which they were kept in anxiety, and as it were bound; and this even to despair: which was also shown me to the life. If anyone comes to them, who is of another genius, and therefore disagrees as to the affections and the thoughts thence, they order him to go away; and when he goes, he everywhere finds the gates closed: on which account he is led to other gates that he may go out, but he still finds them closed: and in the meantime they breathe into him a longing to go out; and this is done until he becomes so weary, that he can no longer endure it; and only then is he let out: and when let out he does not return, on account of the vexation into which he has been driven. The Dutch, more than the rest in the Christian world, know what fantasy is, and what reality; so that they cannot be deluded, like others.

It is not allowed to speak anything with them about religion; wherefore, when anyone comes to them from another religion, he is examined, not by the living voice, and by oral answer; but without his knowledge they explore his thoughts, and draw therefrom what is with them. It has likewise been given to speak with the priests; and I have spoken with them concerning the Lord from the Heavenly Doctrine; and they acknowledged the truths, and were affected. They were then in enlightenment from the Lord. From these things it was granted me to know, that they have a perception of truth above others, both spiritual and civil; and that they look out prudently for themselves, and that this is implanted in them.

In their cities, the men dwell at one side of the city, and the women at the other: and when the men desire, they send to them, and the women come; who are indignant at this, that they are thus to come at the command of the man. And they who in the world had ruled over their husbands, when the like is not given them, being kindled with indignation, wish to go out of the city. They are also sent out; but when they are outside of the city, there appears to them everywhere some obstruction and closure, now marshy, now watery, now something else. Thus they wander, and for a long time seek for places of getting away, and this even to fatigue: wherefore they are compelled to return into the city; and they enter their house, and so are amended. The reason is, that the desire of ruling in marriage takes away conjugial 22-1 love; which increases with a consort as the love of ruling decreases. In place of this then comes love, and with love enjoyment of life; and then neither the man nor the wife, but the Lord, rules: hence is happiness in marriages.

The Dutch appear clothed with coats and breeches altogether as in the world; and they are distinguished from others by the fact that their human derives more from the world than the human of others: for the spiritual does not shine through so clearly as with others. This they derive from their love for business in the world, and thence their continual thought and speculation about it. Even when they come into the spiritual world, they revolve similar things in the mind, and look around on all sides to see where there is trading, and what its quality is: for there is trading in the spiritual world equally as in the natural world; but still the difference is such that it can scarcely be described; and what I wondered at, when they meet with business men who wish to search into their thoughts and intentions secretly by close inspection, as is done there, they forthwith become invisible; which is from this, that they were unwilling in the world to divulge their business to others.

All, whosoever come among spirits after death, are prepared either for heaven or for hell, everyone according to the life formed from doctrine. The preparation is made with most by instructions from the angels. But the Dutch cannot be prepared for heaven and for receiving the spiritual of heaven, which is also the spiritual of the angels, by means of information, for they do not receive it; for they remain more constantly than all others in their faith. When they are informed, they still think from themselves against it. Therefore they are prepared in another manner. Heaven is described to them as to its quality, it is then granted them to ascend into heaven, and see it; and whatever agrees with their genius is insinuated into them, so that they return with the full desire of coming into heaven. But when they are sent back, they are reduced to misery, and business is taken away from them, until they see themselves reduced to extremities, and then they are led around to those who abound in all things, and who are rich; and then the thought is borne upon them what the quality of these is, and how they can be in such abundance, and in the delight of life. They thus reflect upon the life of these, that it is a life of mutual love; also upon their doctrine, that it is the doctrine of that love; and that all their good and pleasant things are from the Lord: and then they are not informed, but inquire themselves, and inform themselves, and thus think from themselves, that in order to get out of their misery they also must believe and do in like manner: and as they receive that faith, but of themselves through the life, abundance is then given them, and so on successively. They are thus prepared for heaven, not by others, but by themselves; not knowing then that they still are not prepared thus by themselves, but by the Lord; because they are such that they also afterwards acknowledge. They are afterwards more constant also than others, so that they may be called constancies; nor do they suffer themselves to be drawn away by any deceit, or by any art, or by reasoning, or by obscurity from insinuated doubts and from sophistries, or by any fallacy, appearance, or fantasy: especially they whose life's love was business, and not money; and whose end was not a sumptuous life.

CALVIN. It was said of Calvin, that he lived a Christian life, and did not place religion in faith alone, as Melancthon and Luther did; and that therefore he is in heaven.

Calvin was seen in a society of heaven, in front above the head, but not in the middle of it; and he said that he was in a like doctrine of the church, in which he was in the world. He told me, that he did not agree with Luther, nor with Melancthon, upon faith alone; since faith and works are so often named in the Word, and are commanded to be done; and that faith and works are therefore to be conjoined: but that Luther felt that if works were admitted, they would not recede far from the papists; but he believed that faith produces works, as a tree does fruit. Calvin is accepted in his society, because he is upright and does not make a disturbance; this I heard from one of the governors of the society.

MELANCTHON. I have spoken with Melancthon and with others concerning him. After he came into the spiritual world, Melancthon confirmed himself in faith alone more than before, so that he was scarcely willing to hear of charity, and of its good: and as he could not persuade any others but those who had led a life scarcely Christian, he therefore procured to himself a persuasive power; which is such that the speech flows into the thought of another, and thus binds it; so that the man is deprived of the power of thinking anything but what is said, though it be false. It fascinates the mind; on which account it is forbidden there; for it extinguishes all light of the understanding; and those whom he could not convince by reasonings, he looked into their eyes, and infused such a persuasion into their minds, that they could not see the falsities nor the sophistries, thus could not answer; on which account they complained about him. This he also tried with me, but with a fruitless effort. Leeks and the smell of them or garlic correspond to this persuasive power; which smell, by its pungency, hurts the left eye. I spoke with him concerning the power of persuasion, and concerning the Nephilim who were in it; who could almost kill a man by their persuasion; concerning which see in the Arcana Coelestia.

There came to me afterwards, from the northern quarter toward the west, certain spirits among the more cunning and malicious; and among them one, who was distinguished from the others by his heavy gait: it was a gait sounding like a bear's. He did many things maliciously; nor did I know who he was. It was afterwards disclosed that he was Melancthon. And that I might know that it was he, he asked where Luther was; and when it was told, he entered in to him, and spoke before him, and was recognized. It was said by Luther, that he spoke much with him about faith alone, or faith separate from good works. Luther inquired of him, what his lot now was: and he disclosed that he was by turns in a chamber paneled above, and by turns in hell under a judge: that when he was in the chamber, he was clothed in a skin like a bearskin, by which he protected himself from the cold; and that he wrote much about faith alone; that when he was in hell under the judge, he was held vile like the rest, and I heard the judge speak of him, that there he was evil, and was sometimes punished for his wicked deeds.

It was further said, that in that chamber the walls are of stone only, without decorations, as elsewhere; and thus it is rude and sad there. On which account, when any, because of his reputation in the world, wish to meet him and speak with him, he does not admit them, because he is ashamed of the rude things there. He sometimes acknowledges that he has been in falsities, and that thence he is such: on which account he sometimes prays that in his chamber he may write concerning charity, and its goods, which are called good works; and then some things are dictated to him from heaven by angels; and when he writes them, the chamber begins to be adorned with various decorations. But after he has written them, and left them upon the table, and read them over, he does not see them; and what he sees, he does not understand; and then the decorations of the chamber vanish: such is his lot.

I heard him speaking with Englishmen out of his paneled apartment. He spoke of faith alone. They said that they do not know what faith alone is. He said that God the Father sent His Son, who suffered for our sins. They said that this is historical: what besides? He said that by that faith they have eternal life. They said, "Did he have eternal life?" To this he could not answer. They said, moreover, that they hear preachers of faith alone, and of justification by it; and when they are hearing, the preaching sounds as if full of wisdom, because it is a well arranged and ingenious composition. But when they come home, they know nothing of what they have spoken, not comprehending their arcana.

I afterwards saw Melancthon among many who held to faith alone, in the place where they are separated, everyone at length goes to the place of his life; and I then heard a voice to them from heaven, that that faith saves no one, because there is nothing of the life in it, nor is there truth in it. On which account they asked, what truth is, and what life is. It was answered that truth and life is to live according to the commandments of the Decalogue: as not to steal, that is, not to act insincerely and unjustly; not to commit adultery; not to kill, or thus, not to burn with deadly hatred and revenge against anyone; not to testify falsely, thus not to lie and defame: and that he who does not do these things because they are sins, has life; and many more truths are afterwards given to him, what evil is, and what good is: and that no other one can be led by the Lord, and be saved; and that it may thence be known, that life and truth are one, as love and faith are; for life is of love, and truth is of faith.

LUTHER. There are places where they contend about religious affairs. Outside of these places their contentions are heard as the gnashing of teeth: and when they are viewed within, it appears as if they were tearing off each other's garments; and their sphere causes pain to the flesh of the teeth and the gums. There came one to me therefrom, with a religious garb, like a monk; and it was said that it was Luther. And he spoke with me, saying that he wished to be among such as contend about things to be believed; because he has brought with him from the world a persuasiveness of speech, and an authority from the consent of many of his time. I observed that he had communication with those who believe that they know all things, and that nothing at all is hidden from them, and who do not wish to learn, but to teach; often saying that is the truth, and that it cannot be contradicted. Such take away from others all freedom of speaking, by inducing their opinions as if they were from God, and by infesting all who contradict, unless for the sake of information. He said that he loves to reason about faith, and likewise about the good of charity; but that he rarely finds those with whom he could be in that delight, for the reason that he had hatched that doctrine from his thought, and that he is thence in the connection of things. It is otherwise with those who only learn it, and afterwards confirm it; they cannot be in such delight, because they are not in such connection of things. He said that they did not long endure his ardor of speaking, but withdraw.

It was given to speak with him concerning faith and love, concerning truth and good, and concerning their marriage, that no more is given from the one than from the other, consequently no more from faith than from life. I spoke with him for two hours with ideas from spiritual light, which are very many; and angelic spirits were then associated with him, for the sake of interior perception: and being at length convinced, he said that he wished to receive that doctrine; but that he doubted whether he could, before the principles respecting faith alone were cast out; which is a matter of labor; on which account also, when he went away, he returned to them, with whom he reasoned as before.

But the angels said that there was some hope of him; because as often as he had thought from his spirit in the world, that is, when left to himself in tranquillity, he had thought about good works, and made them a matter of religion; and it was thence that he spoke so much and wrote so much concerning the good of life, though he did not make it a part of his doctrine, nor to be done for the sake of eternal life; since man cannot do good from himself; and if he does, it is for the sake of heaven, and is a matter of merit. But yet, when he came out of the thought of his spirit into discourse with others, he then, as if turned round, spoke concerning faith alone. He does in like manner at this day. This was the reason that he rejected from the Word the Epistle of James, and also Revelation.

Some have two states, the one when in discourse from doctrine, the other when he thinks with himself. In the former state he is in the body and in its wakefulness, because he is in the lower thought of the speech, and is then in the pleasure of speaking, and for the most part in the pride of learning: but in the latter state he is in his spirit, and then in obscurity, because he thinks within the body, and above the thought next to the natural sensual. This was the case with Luther. He was in the pleasantness of his life, because in the pleasantness of glory, when he was speaking; and this was about faith alone, from his doctrine: but when he was deliberating with himself, he was in favor of good works. Such thought by himself in obscurity remained to him from boyhood, because he was born in that religion, and was a monk. But as he hatched out a new 1 he undertook to withdraw from that religion, by the separation of faith from good works.

Luther related that when he was in the world, it was told him by an angel from the Lord, that he should beware of faith alone, because there was nothing in it; and that for some time he guarded against it, and recommended works: but that he still continued afterwards to separate faith from works, and to make it alone essential and saving.

After Luther was informed by the angels, that no one has any faith unless he has the good of life; and that he has just so much of faith as he has of the good of life, and has no more of the one than of the other; and as he was many times convinced of it: he repented and labored with all his might to get out of the falsities, because he could not come into heaven until he did. I perceived several times that he had repented of it, and that he was laboring against his principles, but still in vain. He also prayed to the Lord that he might be able to recede from his falsities; and he received the answer, that it would be given, if he could receive it. On which account he was sent from one society to another, where those were with whom life was conjoined to faith; but still he could not tarry long, because it was contrary to the delight of his life. It was said to him, that truths of doctrine cannot be received by the life before falsities are rejected, because truths cannot enter where falsities fill the thoughts of the understanding; and that these cannot be easily removed. The reason is, because a man, while he lives in the world, conjoins himself to societies according to the principles of his religion, which had been matters of his affection. In these he likewise remains after death; and in those societies is everyone's life; on which account it is not granted to remove and extricate himself from them, and then betake himself into new ones. It is granted, indeed, as to the thoughts, but it is not granted as to the affections; and yet they act as one. Wherefore the man enters into the new ones; but still withdraws, when he feels undelightful things in the new societies. In a word, Luther sometimes execrates faith alone, and sometimes defends it: he execrates it when he is in fear, and defends it when he is in his love.

ZINZENDORF AND THE MORAVIANS. Zinzendorf. I spoke with Zinzendorf after his death, and then his life, his life's affection, and his principles of religion were disclosed; for a spirit can be let into such a state, that he keeps silence upon absolutely nothing, but lays all things open. It was then laid open, That he had been the greatest persuader; and that he persuaded by asseverations that he knew the arcana of heaven; and that no one comes into heaven but he who is of his doctrine. That at first he spoke with others according to their religion, thus simulating and thus alluring; and that he afterwards implanted his own secrets by first examining well whether they would be received and concealed. It was said that the mystery of his faith had been, that the Lord was born that He might be the adopted Son of God; and that he had at first believed that the Lord was simply the adopted Son of God, [because He had taken on Himself the passion of the cross]; thus that he was an Arian. That he had believed that His Divine was like the divine as with others; but now that it was something more. He hardly wished to hear about the Lord's conception from the Divine, as related in Matthew and Luke; but turned himself away, and was unwilling to say what he felt; and that this is the mystery which they are afraid to manifest. That he attributed sins to the Lord, and said that in the Evangelists He did not speak better than another man, calling them obscure things: that he cared nothing for the Old Testament, and was not willing to hear that the things written there are concerning the Lord. That he rejects all the life of charity, and says it is execrable to think of God and of salvation and the rest as to the life; and that faith separate from charity saves. He believed that he alone with his followers would come into heaven; and that these alone were living, and the rest dead. They speak of themselves what the Lord did of Himself, namely, that they are sons of God; that they are without sins; that they are life and truth; because there is not any evil regarded with those who are in faith: and that for that reason they are life and truth, and call their life blameless because they live by faith.

Still they love the Lord, since to love Him is commanded, because He suffered the cross to propitiate the Father; which is the faith that saves them.

Because he believed that he alone with his followers were to come into heaven, abundant opportunity was given him to ascend into the heavens; and wherever he was, he was ordered to go away, because they perceived from him falsities together with the delight of glory, from the fact that he had established a church. It was perceived that there was merit in the delight of glory. He also spoke with his brethren about heaven; they said that it is not heaven to them.

A spirit appeared to me in vision, bearing a stag in bonds; but which burst the bonds, and rushed with fury against those he met, wishing to lacerate and destroy them. But there then appeared an enormous dog, which, rushing upon the stag, lacerated him, and tore him to pieces. The stag was afterwards seen in the human form, —it was Dippel who [appeared thus,] because he was not allowed to go about refuting all from the delight of his life, and at the same time to excite disturbance. And Zinzendorf said that he had loved him, but that he had observed that he afterwards receded; and that he was such that he wished to lacerate all by his malignant writings; and that he could refute ingeniously, as if full of science and wisdom; and that this gift was natural to him; but that of himself he thought foolishly concerning things.

Zinzendorf, when he first came into the spiritual world, began to wander around to societies and preach, as he had done in the world. But it was said that he was nowhere received, and was conducted away to his Moravian adherents, and perceived that they were not in heaven, but were in misery, because they contemptuously rejected all uses of life, which are good works; when they wish to receive truths, falsities oppose which cannot be dispersed, because they have loved them exceedingly. They know how to falsify the Word and to twist it from its genuine sense in a dexterous and skillful manner; which is done when gathered in an assembly. Some of their attempts against their companions were disclosed, who wished to disprove those mysteries, or also to reveal them; and Zinzendorf said that he therefore removed himself from them. They say that the Lord is to be loved on account of the passion of the cross, but that He is not to be worshipped. They call the Holy Supper a reminder of the passion.

Zinzendorf was in an abstract idea, thinking within himself concerning the Lord. It was observed that he thought of the Lord as of another man, and not that He is God; and that the Divine in Him was as the Divine in another man; and that the Lord spoke in a very simple manner, and not wisely; and that Paul spoke more wisely: but it was shown him that all the Lord's words were words of life, because in each one of them there is a spiritual sense; thus that each one of His words filled heaven, because He spoke by correspondences.

He believed that all things were of mercy, and that if a brother commits a grievous sin, this is remitted to him, because to God that is the means of mercy: that they are altogether condemned; and that it is better for Sodom and Gomorrah than for those who do good works for the sake of salvation; and that this is the sin of sins, because they claim to themselves the merit which is God's alone.

When Zinzendorf was rejected wherever he came, as he saw his Moravian adherents in an unhappy state, he suffered himself to be convinced that he was in falsities, and for that reason labored with all his might and still labors to disperse his falsities, and to receive truths in their stead: but he confessed that he could not tear himself away from the societies in which he inserted himself while in the world; because every man is one with them, nor can he afterwards dissociate himself: for this is meant by the Lord's words respecting the five foolish virgins, that they afterwards wished to buy oil, and likewise bought it; but still could not enter into the wedding.

THE MORAVIANS. That the Arians induce pain in the right arm, near the shoulder blade; but the Socinians induce pain in the breast bone.

The Moravians conceal their mysteries of mysteries, and close up the ways, lest they should be known by others; insinuating themselves through such things from the Lutheran doctrine as agree, proclaiming that they are the remains of the Apostolic Church, who call themselves brethren; and that they have mothers, and certain statutes from the early Christians; but as to the interiors of religion they differ from them altogether. They do not acknowledge the Divine of the Lord as anything else than what is with any other man who is in that faith. They speak lightly of the Word of the Old Testament, and reject it as of no use. The Gospels they do not care for, only Paul's Epistles. They condemn the goods of charity or good works, as to salvation, professing faith separate from charity more than others. Because they are Arians, I spoke with them concerning the Lord. They said that He was sent by God the Father, that by the passion of the cross He might save the human race, and on account of it was acknowledged as a Son, and called the Son of God; that their faith is confidence, that they love the Lord as the best man, because He took upon Himself to propitiate the Father by the passion of the cross. They say that the Lord has power in heaven, and not over heaven. They call Him the Lamb, nor do they ever adore Him as God. When it is said to them, that He was conceived of God, that He says He was from eternity, and that the Father and He are one, they hear these things, but they think against them. They dare not say that it was so written, but was not said: and such things concerning the Lord they miserably distort, and as it were lacerate. They therefore take refuge in these words, that they themselves know how it is, but it is among their mysteries of mysteries.

They call only themselves who are of that faith alive, and all others who are not in that faith, dead; and they believe that they themselves are saved above all others, and that they are to come into the third heaven: but when they come into the first or lowest heaven among the angels, they do not endure the heavenly sphere there, which is derived especially from the goods of charity, and so far from faith; and they therefore flee away thence. Their aversion for that sphere has been perceived and felt by me. And moreover, in no heavenly society are they tolerated, because they think within themselves that all others but they are dead; thus also they have a dead idea concerning the angels themselves. If they come into the second heaven, and especially into the third, where love and charity, and thence the works of charity make the all of heaven, they are seized with pain as those who lie in the death struggle; and lividness comes over their eyes, and they make convulsive motions, and are tortured inwardly.

They have preached much that they have a certain interior sensation and perception, which they say is from an influx from God the Father through heaven, by means of angels or spirits. But it was told them, that they have that sensation or perception from spirits who were Moravians in the world, and that they are in the midst of them, and that these flow in from similar principles, and confirm; which is done strongly, because they love their religious persuasion and think much about it. This was shown them to the life; also that the Quakers are in society with Quaker spirits, Enthusiasts with enthusiastic spirits, and every man with spirits who make one with the affections, and the thoughts or principles taken therefrom; and that it is never otherwise. On account of the living experience they could not but affirm this, though they were unwilling.

The good which they do to the brethren of their assembly they call the good of friendship; and they have something of hatred against those who preach good works.

Footnotes

9-1 The author of The Whole Duty of Man. See SE 5058; CLJ 46.

9-2 The Exhortation is not quoted here. See T 722:3.

12-1 Tafel has, "aedificium;" in the MS. the words, "ubi etiam aedificium est," are written above the line. Possibly it should read, "ubi etiam editius est," "where, also, it is more elevated."

22-1 Tafel has conjugalem; but the MS. has conjugialem.

Because they observe that no one can come into heaven except those who acknowledge the Divine of the Lord, and they cannot do this, they recede from love towards the Lord on account of the passion of the cross, and act as one with the infernals. From that hatred they have it with themselves as it were implanted, that they persecute the angelic spirits in ways sometimes nefarious; but they are severely punished.

They rarely hold companionship with others: they appeared at first to the right in the plane of the knees; but by turns they were diminished, cast off, and scattered. Among themselves they speak of their mysteries with closed doors, and severely prohibit the revelation of these mysteries unless by general consent; yea, they threaten: whether from those threats something has broken forth in the world; they were not willing to be explored, what they had done against some.

They call all things with them, when in their faith and confidence, holy.

There flows out from their sphere a perception of heinous adultery, because they adulterate the Word throughout, and likewise mock at many things therein.

They appeared to the left in the plane of the foot, where it was disclosed that they made one with the evil, against those who have been in the goods of charity, and acknowledged the Divine of the Lord; all of whom are angelic spirits; and become angels: wherefore they were driven away towards the north. But because they were there not willing to become quiet, but that they would plot evil, calling to their aid the Babylonians, on this account they were driven still more remotely into the north, and sent into a cavern, which tended obliquely under the west, that they might no longer injure others. They form a brotherhood everywhere.

They were compelled to an interior confession of the Lord; and I then heard profane things, such as I should scarcely dare to publish; denying, yea, profaning the things which are said there concerning the conception of the Son by the Father; that He was carried away from the sepulcher by the disciples; that the transfiguration was a vision induced by fantastic spirits; that He was a man so low that He was lower than others; besides more heinous things from which it was evident that they are the worst of all in Christendom, and that they have hatched a theology out of their skull, and have afterwards consulted the Word, profaning it, because it does not make one with their vain delusions. The evils with themselves they call goods, because [they say] nothing of evil is imputed to them.

They were afterwards called together, and were explored whether they were all unanimous in professing those heinous things; and it was found that some of them had not such a heinous dogma; who were they that were ignorant of those mysteries. They constituted one-third part of them: these were separated; and the rest when separated were given to certain ones as servants: and it was forbidden them to thus gather together anymore. The rest also were separated, and sent into societies, with the prohibition that they should not be together. The Holy Supper they did not make holy. Concerning Baptism, they have it in use on account of the Reformed.

The rest were gathered together into congregations, and after visitation were cast down towards the lower parts, and were compelled to enter a cavern.

But because they had no food there, but vile chambers, they complained loudly; and were sent forth, and cast out into the deserts. Zinzendorf saw this.

THE QUAKERS. When other spirits wish to explore what they think, they conceal their thoughts in a certain way, saying that it is enough that they do no evil to anyone, nor openly speak evil of anyone. But it was said to them, that not to speak evil of anyone is a good in an earthly society; but that to think ill of others injures society in the other life, because there the ideas of thought are communicated. They do not wish to be instructed in doctrinals. They answer, "I do not understand this: What is this?" They have often affirmed that they have been taught by the Holy Spirit, and that they are taught. They most stubbornly resist, to prevent anything of their arcana from being published. The spirits who are with Quakers, whom they think to be the Holy Spirit, are they who were of the same sect in the world. To these after death they first pass; who inspire into them not to promulgate anything; wherefore they live separated; they are spurious spirits. 59-1 A communion of certain detestable wives was disclosed: they then expect an influx from the holy spirit, with a perception of leave that it is permitted. Their secret holy worship consists of such things, and by such things also the communication of their holy is effected. They do not at this day have the trembling and the total shaking, as formerly; but an uncertain shaking on the left side of the body and face. When they assert that it is commanded by the holy spirit, no one objects to adulteries and whoredoms. I spoke with their founder, who said that he never did such things, nor thought them. It was seen that Quaker spirits live in dense forests, like wild hogs: they become fantastic spirits. Those were also seen who believe that they are born holy, although he be one born from their adultery; respecting whom the rest say, that he alone drinks red wine in heaven; which wine they call celestial. But he appeared like a heinous man, and became black, and appeared to the angels like mucus of the nose. Such, dissociated, sit in their own places, like barks and the lees of oil, for ages. After those ages they retain very little of life, and serve societies for a vile connection. I spoke with Penn, who asserted that he was not such, and that he took no part in such things. It was said that the first of them were enthusiastic spirits, who are such that they wish to possess man. Those who from the dullness of the understanding wish to be called a holy spirit, are more corporeal as it were than the others. They say that they not only speak from the holy spirit, but also eat with the holy spirit; and that with some the spirit is infused into their feasts.

THE SAINTS OF THE PAPISTS. The papists, especially the monks, when they come into the other life, inquire for the saints, each one for those in his order; and the Jesuits do the same: and they likewise find them; but when they speak with them, they do not find more of holiness with them than with others. On being questioned, they say that they have no more power than others; and that they who have not worshipped the Lord, but only the Father, have no power; and that they are among the vile, whom their associates despised. Some of them know that they have been canonized; and when they are proud of it, they are derided by their associates; some do not know it. The most of those who affected sanctity in the world, are in the lower earth and in the hells, because they did this from the insane love, that they wished to be invoked and worshipped as gods; and that love profanes all the sanctity of heaven. But still the monks, and especially the Jesuits, conceal the lot of those, and lie to the common people, that they are saints on account of a restraint 60-1 and obedience; although they laugh at them in their hearts. 60-2

I heard the Pope who lived in the year 1738, -because he receded from the Babylonish error, and renounced all power over souls and over heaven, and became a Christian, calling upon the Lord alone, 61-1 he related to me that he had spoken with almost all who had been made saints, of both sexes; and, except two, he had seen no one in heaven; and that these two abhorred being invoked: and that many of them were not aware of it; and that some spoke foolishly.

St. Genevieve. She appears sometimes to the Parisians, in a middle altitude, in a splendid dress, and then as it were with a saintly face, and grants herself to be seen by many. But when some begin to invoke her, then immediately her face changed, and also her garments; and she becomes like another woman, and chides them, and rebukes them severely, for wishing to worship a woman, whose lot is no other than the lot of ordinary women, and who is not more highly esteemed among her associates than others: and she chides them even to shame, that men in the world are taken with such trifles. I will add, that the reason why she appears to them such at the beginning, was to the end that it might be known what kind of delusions these were. I heard the angels say that she sometimes appears so, for the sake of separating the worshippers of men from the worshippers of God. She also teaches them that she knows nothing at all more than others, and nothing whatever about invocation.

She says also that she is not among the best; and that he who wishes to become greater than others, becomes lower than others; and that it is an injury to the most of them that they have been canonized; because, when they hear of it, they become puffed up in heart from hereditary evil, and are removed away, that they may not know at all who they were in the world.

Agnes dwells in a chamber with virgins for her companions; and as often as she is called forth by any worshipper, she goes out, and asks what they want with a shepherd girl, who in herself is low, and is one with others in their work. And then her companions go out, and chide them even to shame. And as soon as they are ashamed, and desist from such things, she is also guarded, lest pride should enter into her. But she is now conducted away to another place; nor is she found anymore to the right among the upright women; in whose society she is not tolerated, unless she answers that she is filthy.

The saints adored in the world are of three kinds. Some are averse to the worship; these are guarded by angels. Some orally repudiate it, but still cherish in heart that they wish to be worshipped. Some receive it; but these are profane, miserable, and foolish.

Anthony of Padua appeared to me in front a little below, at the plane of the foot. He appeared in a dark garment; and I spoke to him as to whether he supposed he was a saint. He at first answered that he was not at all a saint: but still it was perceived that he retained the pride, that he wished to be one; on which account I spoke with him more severely. When anyone comes to him, he is led to say, that he can introduce no one into heaven, and that he knows nothing at all about being invoked; that this is a falsity. When they inquire of him what heaven is, whether it is the Lord, and whether it is love from Him and to Him and mutual love, this he does not know: on which account other spirits, from whom he wishes to get away, and cannot, mock at him. An interior craftiness has been observed in him. He endeavors to be worshipped in secret ways; but he fears: for he would be thrust down to lower places, where he suffers hard things. He can by art bind the ideas of the thought of others. He has conjunction with the Jesuits who appear in white.

Francis Xavier dwells deep beneath the back parts. He was a subtle magician, operating through conjugial love and through innocence; thus clandestinely.

Ignatius was in front above. He was a good spirit. He said that he was averse to being canonized, making himself filthy. He detested their making saints. He knew about the Jesuits, and called them atheists, and said that he shunned them.

The Virgin Mary, the mother of the Lord, was seen. Mary appeared to one side, in a snow-white garment, only as she passed by: and then she stopped a little, and said, that she had been the mother of the Lord; that He was indeed born of her; but that He became God, and put off all the maternal human; and that she therefore now adores Him as her God; and that she is unwilling that anyone should acknowledge Him as her son, because in Him all is Divine.

MOHAMMED AND THE MOHAMMEDANS. See some things concerning the judgment upon the Mohammedans, and that there are two Mohammeds under the Christian heaven, in the small work on the Last Judgment .

That a choir is when many speak and act together and unanimously, and that by choirs inauguration to unanimity is made and that in their speech there is singing, see in the Arcana Coelestia.

Mohammed. I have spoken with the Mohammed, who is in his stead, who had his seat under the Christian heaven: it seemed as if the glory of the Lord was shown to the Mohammedans, and that they then fell down upon their faces; and their Mohammed did the same.

I have heard the Mohammedans speak so skillfully and prudently as to affect certain Christian spirits with shame, acknowledging Mohammed but adoring the one only Lord of the universe: and Mohammed then testified that he has no power, and he also then adored the Lord.

I have sometimes seen that Mohammed drive away from himself the crowd that adores him, saying that they should go to the Lord, who rules the universe.

Spirits were sent to me from Mohammed, who could induce the appearance of a laver, pleasant through the form of its flow.

Both Mohammeds confess that the Lord is the fountain of all goodnesses and truths.

The spirits who are around Mohammed are inaugurated into unanimity and into agreement by angelic choirs, to the end that they may suffer themselves to be acted upon, and to think, will and speak from the Lord through angels; (respecting choirs see above;) and I have seen and heard them present by them beautiful representations concerning the Lord, the Savior of the world. The work of choirs is performed by Mohammedans with great merit. The Mohammedan choirs there became more familiar to me than others. I was with Mohammed on a remarkable occasion: it was also when I was in

Amsterdam, and in the courthouse there, which he saw through my eyes, and praised. He was delighted with the marbles there, which marbles correspond to the affections of the Mohammedans, who are in some degree spiritual; for all things are correspondences. Golden things correspond to the affections of the angels of the third heaven; things of silver to those of the second; things of copper to those of the first; and India porcelain to those of the last: to those of the Mohammedan heaven things of marble.

The two Mohammeds were once taken up into heaven, because they desired it; and they then spoke with me therefrom. They said that they saw thence, in one idea of thought, innumerable things, which, when below heaven, they believed to be one single thing: this was done, that they might know how the Lord leads man by innumerable things, which in the natural state appear to the man as one; when yet there are ineffable things in every one of them. This may be compared with the least things of an animalcule, which appears to the naked eye as one obscure point, but seen under a powerful microscope, is yet an animal endowed with members, and likewise with organs, and within with muscles, fibers, heart, brain, and many other things. So it is with one idea of a man's thought; therefore no one but the Lord alone knows what kind of thought the man has, and how much of what is living, that is, of heaven, there is in him: for as much of heaven as there is in him, so much of the human there is in him from the Lord. These things the two Mohammeds learned by being elevated into heaven.

There were Mohammedans in the western quarter dwelling upon rocks, who were rejected by the Mohammed in the Christian region, because they worshipped Mohammed as God, and adored him; which was forbidden them: and it was found that then they thought nothing respecting the Lord, not even respecting Him as the greatest Prophet, and the Son of God. And when it was inquired what kind of idea they had concerning God the Father, and it was found that they not only had not the idea of Him as a man, but none at all, and without an idea of God there is not given conjunction with any heaven; it was said to them that they could rather have the idea of God respecting the Lord, because He was the greater Prophet, and the Son of God: but they said that they could not, for He was of a wandering nation. Since they worshipped Mohammed, therefore Mohammed himself, who wrote the Koran, and was buried at Mecca, was taken from his place, which was to the right deeply behind the right foot, and he was elevated a little above the earth, and was shown to them. He appeared gross and black, altogether similar to corporeal spirits, who have little of life. He spoke with them, confessed that it was he, and that he was such: and after he had been shown, he was carried down into his place; but those worshippers of Mohammed were dispersed.

It was afterwards disclosed whence were the two Mohammeds, who had obtained a seat in the Christian heaven: because one of them was born in Saxony, and taken by the Algerians; and he there adopted the Mohammedan religion, and became a ship captain. He was then taken by the Genoese, where he received the Christian religion: thus he became imbued with both religions, because he acknowledged the Lord: and being led by the love of ruling, he was therefore taken there instead of Mohammed, and infused into the Mohammedans the belief that he was Mohammed himself: he was clever.

[Marginal Note:] I have heard that Mohammed say that he acknowledges the Lord as the only God, in whom is the Father, who is one God with Him: and that the Holy proceeding from Him is the Divine filling the heavens, and making the heavens.

But the other Mohammed was disclosed as being a Christian from Greece. He was also acknowledged by those who in the world had thought of many Mohammeds.

With the first Mohammed there appears something luminous, as if from a little torch; and the Mohammedans look thither, and there is influx thence into then through the medium of spirits: for in the spiritual world distances are only appearances; and when anyone is thought of, the distance perishes, and there becomes presence; Mohammed is skillful in instructing those who inquire of him. It has been granted me to perceive the sphere of his life: it was exteriorly pleasant, but interiorly concealing lasciviousness, which they have from matrimony with many wives and concubines. It was an unclean heat, but which is a pleasant heat, to the Mohammedans.

The reason that Mohammeds are continually substituted in place of another, is because everyone after death is led into his religious persuasion which he had in the world: it is a continuation of life. But he is afterwards gradually led away either to goods or to evils, according to his life; according to which also he receives truths or falsities.

THE MOHAMMEDANS I was conducted to a region where the Mohammedans were, which region was towards the right in the plane of the sole of the right foot: and when I was there, I was held in the thought concerning the Lord, that the Father is in Him, and He in the Father; and that the Holy Spirit proceeds; thus in the thought that there is one God, in whom is a trine. All those who were there were then in the same idea, and altogether acknowledged it; and this through all that tract. It was thence granted me to know, that there are many from the Mohammedans who receive the belief concerning the Lord, that He is one with the Father.

When I was conducted by the Lord through all the places, that I might know the quality of those there from their various nations, I came also to two mountains, upon which were Mohammedans. On one were those who lived well morally; they said that they have good, because they obey their governors. On the other were those who were very perceptive of spiritual things. They stated at first that no others can come to them but they who are of a like genius; and that Christians cannot; and that if they come, they appear to them as if they were being swallowed up by wolves; and that those who still come, they send to prison, and treat badly, and afterwards dismiss: these are monks who are able to introduce themselves by their arts, but are detected. I spoke with them respecting many wives; and they heard the reasons why it is according to the Christian doctrine, that only one wife is to be received. They perceived the justice in the reasons, but answered that they cannot as yet recede from matrimony with many, because it was conceded to them by their religion in the world, for the reason that they are orientals, who, without many wives, would have burned forth into adulteries, and so would have perished.

I spoke also with the firstborn of the Christians, who are the military guards of their Sultan, called Janizaries, and became Mohammedans: they said that they were still Christians in heart; and that some were intermediate, but some Mohammedans.

When I spoke something from the Word with those who were upon the other mountain, I apperceived something holy from them: as when I said that the Lord was conceived from Jehovah; and for that reason He called Him Father; and it is thence that He is the Son of God; and thence the Divine is in Him; and therefore He could glorify His whole body; so that as to that part of the body, which from those who are born of human parents is rejected and putrefies, was with Him glorified and made Divine from the Divine in Himself; and He rose with this leaving nothing in the sepulcher, altogether otherwise than takes place with every man. They heard attentively and said that they wondered they had not heard of such things.

I saw an infestation of Mohammedans by Christians in a certain city; from which infestation they could with difficulty be rescued. It was done by arts, of which there are many in the spiritual world. It was then seen that the city sank down in the middle part, and there was a wall made round about. But the sinking down was little, so that they could ascend and descend. Thus those who withdrew were transferred, and exempted from the infestations.

I was conducted to the Mohammedans who are in the eastern quarter, and it was granted me to speak with them. They said that some Christians of the Roman Catholic religion come to them; and they observed that it was done by them only for the sake of gain and dominion: and further, that they wish to possess all the things of the world, and also to have dominion over all who are there. There was a conversation with them concerning God: they said that they cannot comprehend how they can perceive one God, when they name three, and call them persons; when yet there is but one God; and that they still heard from the Christians, that they also say one God; because this is a contradiction. They asked what I knew concerning God. I said, that in the Christian heaven that is not believed, nor is it so said: but that the trine is in one Person; and that the trine which is named in it is the Father, the Son, and the Holy Spirit, that this is in the Lord, in whom the inmost, which is the esse of life, is called the Father; the second, which is the existere of life thence, is the Son; and the third is the proceeding, and is called the Holy Spirit: and that such a union was effected by God the Father, by His coming in the world; and that Christians might also be enlightened in it, since the Lord teaches openly, that the Father is in Him, and that the Father and He are one, and that the Holy Spirit does not speak out of itself, but from Him: but they who are of the Roman Catholic religion do not admit this, for the reason that they are lords on the earth; neither the Reformed, who are in the religion of faith alone; for so far the Mohammedans comprehended this. They said that they thought, desiring illustration, which was afterward given them; since this thing cannot be comprehended, without instruction from the Word.

I spoke with the Mohammedans concerning the resurrection; that the Christians believe that the resurrection is first to take place with the destruction of the world; and that the bodies are then to be united to their souls, and to be gathered together from every quarter where they have been scattered; and that in the meantime they are spirits, of whom they have an idea as of wind, especially of the breath; and that thus they flit about either in the ether or in the starry heaven, without hearing, sight, or any other sense; and that they are in expectation of the judgment; and that those also are in this expectation who have died from the very beginning of this earth; who have thus flitted about in the universe now for six thousand years; and that some think that they are together in a certain place, which is not a place, but a somewhere or other; as also that the angels are such. Also that the Christians scarcely comprehend that man lives a man after death as in the world, for they cannot have an idea of the spiritual body; but that still, when they do not think from doctrine, they think of themselves after death, that they live as men, as when they are near to death: and that for that reason those who treat of the deceased write openly that they are among the angels, are speaking with them, are in white garments, in paradises; yet as soon as they come to any ideas from doctrine, they think, as was said, of man after death, and of an angel, as of wind. When these things were said, the Mohammedans then answered, that they wondered that such a fallacy can reign with Christians, who call themselves more enlightened than others; saying that they know that they are to live after death, are to live in happy marriage, and are to drink wine; and this after they have rejected the castoffs, which had served them for their ultimate clothing in that gross sphere, as a body there.

There are many Mohammedans who become Christians, acknowledging the Lord as the only God, because the Father is in Him. These, when they are led into heaven, are led first to the east, and thence to the north, and thence ascend higher and higher to the west, and are there in a higher place; but still by a circuit, or going round, according to situation below; some appeared to ascend towards the south, who were they that confirmed themselves in the Divinity of the Lord.

Many Mohammedans, from natural light, comprehend better concerning spiritual things than the Christians do; because they think much, and desire truths. They understood well that all the things in heaven and in the world refer themselves to good and truth; and that truth, when it is believed, is the truth of faith; and that good, when a man is affected by it, is the good of love: and therefore two faculties, understanding and will, were given to man; the understanding by the reception of truth, thus of faith, and the will by the reception of good, thus of love: and that good and truth, thus the understanding and the will, must be one, that the man may be truly a man; thus also a man of faith and of truth. They clearly perceived thence that they who are in the good of life, are in the perception of truth; for the reason that good desires truth, and wishes to be conjoined, and as it were nourished; and that truth is as spiritual food to good; also on the other hand that truth desires good, that it may be anything; because without good there is no life in truth; thus that there is the reciprocal desire of the one for the other, and that from this man is man.

In the Judgment I saw that the Mohammedans were led from the west and round about in their circuit around the Papists, by a way towards the north to the east, in a circular way to appearance: and that on the way the evil were cast outside of that sphere where there is a space of great extent; some into a wilderness there, some into swamps and pools, some into dark forests. These things were on the backside of their mountain: on the side of that space in the north there was an immense and extended whirlpool, into which also many, who had led an evil life, were cast. The rest proceeded by a circuit towards the east, and spread themselves into an ample space that extended itself more to the back. Thither those were led, who acknowledged God the Father, and the Son as the greatest Prophet, who is with the Father. That space was broad, divided into mountains, hills, and valleys, upon which they were arranged; and there it is well with them. They who were still better, enjoying more intellectual light than others, were likewise led to that place, where there was communication with the Christian heaven, a space which separated intervening. These were they, who, being instructed, received the Lord; and they who received well, were led into the south, where they obtained their heaven behind the Christians there.

There were those who feigned themselves Christians as to the belief in the Lord's Divinity. These insinuated themselves among them by craftiness, but were forthwith detected and separated, and cast into the desert and the adjoining chasm; and some were led back and dispersed.

There were some from the Mohammedans who acknowledged only the Father as others do, and the Lord as the greatest Prophet. They said that they could not understand that the Divine is divided into three Persons, thus into three gods. They said that the Holy Spirit was God speaking by a spirit, and an angel; a certain one from the Christians now drew near to them, asking why they do not acknowledge the Son of God as God. They said that there is one God, and thus there would be two; on which account they asked him how many Gods he worshipped; he replied One, because God is one. But they explored the idea of his thought, that he did not think of one God, but of three. This is easily done in the other life. They said that they saw that he said one God with the mouth, and in heart and in faith believed in three: and yet it behooves a Christian to speak as he thinks, and not to divide the mind from the speech, as do flatterers and those who lie; and as he could not deny this, they said that the Christians ought to be ashamed to think of three gods, when no Gentile who has any intelligence thinks so; who have not three in their idea, when they name one. He wished to say that the three were one by unanimity; neither could this be given without the idea of three conversing and consenting among themselves; and besides, three essences which make one could not be given, unless they were also one person: one and the same essence of three is not given; still less in God, who is not divisible: and who, moreover, can give it from an essence, such as this is among the metaphysicians, and have it be thought by the common people, when it cannot be by the learned? On which account he was affected with shame, saying that he would in no wise return to them, and that he would inquire of someone concerning the triune God. The angels afterwards spoke with the Mohammedans, instructing them that God is one both in Person and in essence, in whom is a trine; and that the Son of God, who to them is the greatest Prophet, being sent by the Father, cannot but be God, because He was conceived of God the Father Himself: thus the Divine itself was in Him from conception; and the Divine is indivisible.

The mansions of the Mohammedans, after death are palaces. They are for the greatest part in the western quarter. After the Last Judgment there came many anew into that quarter, who thought little respecting the God of the universe, and nothing respecting the Lord, but worshipped Mohammed as God.

And because they did not find him, they elected another, on a mountain elevated above the Christian region, with whom they consulted, and whom they obeyed: and then, by the command of their new Mohammed, they poured themselves into the Christian region, and infested them in various modes. But after visitation, and the disclosure that they were a wandering nation, and one that delighted in idleness, and wished to do nothing useful, they were cast into their hells. As long as they consociated themselves with the Babylonians, they were also able to render themselves inconspicuous. At length the earth upon which they were was rolled over above them, and they were cast into hell: their hell appeared fiery.

. The judgment upon them proceeded still further into the west, in a long tract; and likewise towards the north, where they mingled themselves with the evil Papists; and I saw them cast into the hells and whirlpools there.

Many of the Mohammedans, when they had heard many things concerning the Lord, wished to go and join the heavenly Christian Church. But it was told them that they should remain still in their religion, or in their doctrine from the Koran, that the Lord was the greatest Prophet, the Son of God, the wisest of all, sent to inform the human race; for the reason that they cannot in heart acknowledge His Divine, but only with the month; since they imbibed those things from infancy: and their spiritual good was formed in part from such things as had been of their faith; which cannot be extinguished so suddenly by a new tenet of faith, let them only live in sincerity and justice, and so in their good: because all sincerity and justice is in itself the Divine proceeding from the Lord; and because they can in their manner still live faithfully, and be gradually led on to the Lord. It was said to them, that many Christians do not think of the Lord's Divine, but only of His Human, which they do not make Divine; for instance, the Roman Catholics, as also the Reformed; who for that reason go to the Father, that He will have mercy for the Son's sake and rarely to the Lord Himself: on account of which belief and prayer, they continually retain the idea concerning the Lord, that He is a man like any other.

It was told me that there is a book among the Mohammedans which is common in their hands, in which some pages were written by correspondences, like the Word with us; from which pages there is some light in the heavens.

There were with me many from Greece, who had dwelt in the world with the Mohammedans; complaining that then as well as now they inveighed against them because they worship three Gods; to whom they also replied, that they worship one God, and that the three are one: but they still persist that they are three which they worship, since they name three; and they ask which God of the three they worship the most: and when they reply that they worship all together, they then say that thus there is one God, and the rest are little gods; and that it is only said thus. But when they hear it said that they are equal, they withdraw, and set themselves against the Christians, as having little or no judgment in spiritual things. They complained that they do not give up the infestation, until they say that they are three names of the one God: then they acquiesce. They afterwards inquired respecting the three names of the one God. It was told them from heaven, that the Christians derived those names from the sense of the letter of the Word, where three names of the one God are mentioned: and by the Father is there meant the Creator of the universe; by the

Son, the Savior of the human race; and by the Holy Spirit, enlightenment; and that these three are in the Lord alone; and that in Him the three are one; and that He teaches this in the Word. But on account of the class, who are not willing to regard the Lord's Human as Divine, because they have claimed all His power to themselves, they were not willing to have it said that it is Divine power, and thus that they were gods on the earth; and when it was read to them out of Matthew and Luke, that He was conceived from God the Father, and thus the Divine was in Him, and He was from it; they said that they supposed He was the son of Joseph. And when it was said to them that He did not come into the world to reconcile the human race to the Father, but to conquer the devil, that is, to subjugate the hells, that He might reduce all things [on earth] and in the heavens to order, and might at the same time glorify His Human, or might reunite it to the Divine, which was the soul itself in Him from conception; and that thus and no otherwise could the human race be saved. On hearing these things they were silent, and many acquiesced.

Footnotes

59-1 [MARGINAL NOTE.] There are Quaker spirits who, from their worship by Quakers in the world, believe themselves to be the holy spirit, and to have been from eternity but in process of time they come among the profane who are called stercoracenus and cadaverous spirits, abominable excrement.

60-1 The M.S. has, mucus narium; Tafel, mercurius vivus. See SE 3811, 3812, where mucus narium occurs.

60-2 The M.S. has a marginal note which Tafel omits, namely, Sunt spiritus quaqueriani qui ex cultu a quaqueriis in mundo se credunt spiritum sanctum et ab aeterno fuisse, sed successu temporis veniunt inter prophanos, qui vocantur spiritu stercorei et cadaverosi, excrementum abominabile.

61-1 Clement XII, Pope A.D. 1730-1740.

It was said to them that there are Mohammedans who receive the belief that the Lord is one with the Father, and that they have a heaven in which all things are happy; and that they live there from the Lord in spiritual marriage of good and truth.

SOME THINGS CONCERNING THE PAPISTS. When the Last Judgment was going on, he who was Pope in the year 1738, and was then blind in his old age, dwelt on high near a city in the northern quarter; and I saw him then brought away, and carried sitting upon a litter, and sent into a secure place; and as everyone after death is first led to his own religion, and afterwards is led away from it, as far as he can be, they also, for that reason, seek for the Pope: on which account someone is always appointed, who takes on the name and the function of Pope. He was for a long time in that function after that time; but when he observed that he had no power at all of remitting sins, nor of opening heaven, and that this power was Divine, and thence the Lord's alone, he therefore began to be averse to that doctrine, and afterwards to abhor it, and he abdicated that office, and betook himself among the Christians who worship the one Lord, and is with them in heaven. I have often spoken with him; and he called himself happy, that he had embraced those truths, and had removed himself away from that idolatrous religious persuasion. He said that he revolved in his mind similar things in the world, and acknowledged in heart that the Word was holy, and that the Lord was to be worshipped; but that he could not then recede, on account of causes which he also mentioned.

But it happened otherwise with his successor, Benedict XIV. He declared openly that he had confirmed in his own mind, that since the Lord had transferred all power over the heavens to Peter, He had no power at all left, and no longer any holiness. I saw him speaking with Sextus V, who was called up from below, and after the conversation sank down again. I heard him speaking many things in regard to the Word with someone concerning the Bull Unigenitus, but this is not the place to make them public. He was cunning, and at first civil, and then very sharp-sighted: he loved the Jesuits more than others, and went down to them into their hell; nor have I as yet seen him come up therefrom: and scarcely is he to come up thence, because he said that he had confirmed and established the Bull Unigenitus, and because he said that the Sacred Scripture was not equal in his mind to the papal decree, but inferior to it. When it was shown him that the Word was holy in every word, and that they were perpetual correspondences, and that thence it was for the whole heaven, he made this of no account, saying that the papal decrees were of the same holiness. But then it was said, that there is in each thing which the Pope pronounces in the Consistory, something derived from the infernal love of ruling over heaven and earth, and of ascribing to himself the Divine power, and so of being worshipped as God; and that hell, and not heaven, is in such a decree. And it was shown from what spirits it is said, and who it is that then breathe into and move the breast; that they are infernal spirits, who are not willing to believe in salvation by the Holy Spirit, 103-1 but he reasoned against those things.

Louis XIV, king of France, is at this day among the happy. He was made by the Lord the governor over the best society of the French nation, over those who are arriving in the spiritual world from the world. He acts uprightly and justly, and is diligent in looking out for things useful to his subjects there. He acknowledges the Lord, and that He has power over the heavens and the earth. He reads the Word, and shuns cunning and craftiness. He said that he was such in the world. Once when I was speaking with him, he suddenly descended seemingly as if by steps, to a place below me a little in front; and it was perceived that then in vision he was as if he was at Versailles. And it was then perceived that he had come as if into a kind of sleep; and it immediately became silent around him, and also with me; which lasted two hours. Afterwards he ascended, and spoke to those who stood around him, saying that he had spoken with the king of France, his grandson, who reigns at this day; and that he exhorted him to desist from confirming the Bull Unigenitus; and he said that otherwise misfortune would come upon him. He said that he did not know whether he perceived that in clear vision, or obscure vision, which are in the thought with some emotion of the mind. This took place Dec. 13, 1759, about seven or eight o'clock.

After the Last Judgment, the Babylonians were for a long time gathered together upon mountains in the west as before. The reason is, that a spirit after death can go nowhere else than the place where his life is. They were thus there upon mountains, where a part made to themselves as it were new heavens. But as soon as it was calculated that there were about two hundred there, they were cast down into the hells, as before; and this was done until all things were reduced into such order; and no one after death can go anywhere but into his own hell; nor can a part remain upon the earth there; and this is done when those places are taken possession of by societies, where they are in the acknowledgment and adoration of the Lord. The southern quarter, where the richest were, and where the great city of the Jesuits is, which quarter was altogether overturned, as may be seen from the description of the Last Judgment, is still a desert land; and I saw the monks there sometimes, who, as they had heard that treasures were hidden away there, still flocked thither for the purpose of exploring; but in vain.

Nor do they still desist from sending out their emissaries into the Reformed Christian world, for the purpose of seducing as in the world. They are monks, who thirst solely for gain and who aspire to supreme, yea Divine, power and who are so barren that they know nothing at all of Divine truth; but yet they prevail over others by cunning; nevertheless they are investigated, and those who have been investigated are miserably punished.

It was shown me to the life, why Babel or Babylon was called Lucifer, son of the dawn, Isa. 14 and Gen.. That by Lucifer there Babel is meant, is manifest from what precedes and follows there, concerning which the things there may be quoted. And that Babel in the beginning adored the Lord, and observed the commandments more than others, bearing domination in the mind; but that in process of time domination becomes the head, and at length endeavors to drag the Lord Himself from His throne, and to place itself thereon.

The women and virgins who have lived in convents, and have thought lascivious things, and still more those who have done lascivious things, are cast into hells where there are direful things. But they who have cultivated piety alone, and have not done any work, are divided among the adherents of their own religion, to act as servants, learning that bare piety in idleness does not conduce to salvation. But they who were diligent and loved to work, are allotted places among those women in the churches, with whom it is well. They who have been diligent in the convents, by serving others there in various ways, as to food, clothing, and other functions there, and who did these things from charity and affection, are conducted away beyond that mountain into the confines between the south and west, and form a society, which is protected from infestations from the men, and they are sent to those who teach the truths of faith; for they are more teachable than others.

There was a vast multitude of Papists dwelling to the east, occupying all those mountains, 109-1 even from the eastern quarter to the southern, who introduced themselves to the Gentiles upon the mountains and plains there. All that multitude was transferred by a direct way to the west, where a settlement was given them upon hills and plains for a great extent. They were those who had lived in goods, although not in truths, who had performed good works according to their religion, and were of that genius that they would not injure others, nor plot evils. That they desired truths is manifest from the fact that while they were on the way they appeared as if they were borrowing silver and garments, as the sons of Israel did from the Egyptians; by which was signified that they desired truths, and were receiving them from them; from those who do not do anything good.

The vast multitude was explored as to the quality of its affection of truth from good, and at the same time whether they had lived in the good of charity. That exploration was seen as a sudden and instantaneous transference to various quarters. They who were in the middle remained there; because they were in the affection of truth, and wished to be imbued with the truths of faith. The rest were sent back, that they might first be instructed below by their own people, who had been upright monks, and at the same time had been in some doctrine of truth from the Word; and they were afterwards transferred to those of the Reformed, who, on account of a life according to the truths of the Word, were angelic spirits.

I also saw a vast multitude of the Catholic nation, who had been hidden away and reserved by the Lord for a long time, and were reserved from the idolatrous contagion of the others; because they had lived well, and had acknowledged the Lord: and some were transferred to the south, some to the east, some to the west, and some to the north, that they might form some heavenly society, and be further instructed. For this end angels were sent to them, not only to instruct them, but also to guard them from the cunning and deceitful of their own nation, and from the influx out of their hells. In a word, many and great societies were instituted out of Catholics, and partly inserted into societies where the Word is read freely and the Lord is adored. If, after being instructed, they have received the truths of faith in the good of love, they are elevated thence into heaven. It is not their fault that they were born there. All their infants are in heaven: but these are ignorant of the falsities of their parents, not knowing that they are such; and they are educated under the Lord's auspices by the angels.

The most malicious of the Roman Catholics become the most stupid, for the reason that when malice penetrates all the interiors of the mind, and destroys all spiritual truth, they then first become insane, and afterwards stupid, and are sent under the earth between the west and the north. When anyone passes to that place, great stupor occupies his thought, and torpor his body. Many of them were worshippers of the devil, and had books where the doctrine of the worship of them was contained. One or two of their books were taken from them and read before others. The doctrinal teaching was this: that they petition God the Father to excuse them for betaking themselves to the devil; because they petitioned for help from God the Father, and had not obtained it, knowing that they get help from the devil; on which account they betake themselves to him, calling him their patron. Another book was opened, written with various characters and flexures, and being deciphered, taught that they had nothing from the Divine, but all from the devil. Being asked the reason they said, that they had not obtained from God by prayers their request that they might rule as in the world, over the souls of men and over the goods of that earth. It was told them that no one obtains this by prayers. Being detected, at first they became insane, and were cast down from the mountain on which they were, from the southern side of the mountain, into a direful hell where the worshippers of the devil are; and their houses collapsed together into heaps. One of them ran to me, and he was dusky like a devil.

Those of them who are upright by nature, cannot dwell together with those who have attained spiritual uprightness from the affection of truth; for those who are upright from any natural uprightness are easily seduced. They believe all things, even things of cunning, and adore idols; on which account also they are among those who serve others as handmaids and servants; by whom they are guarded, lest they should be approached by the monks.

THE AFRICANS. There are, among the blackest of the Africans, those who love to be punished and treated harshly; and who come into heaven, saying afterwards that they detest blackness, because they know that their souls are white and their bodies black.

I have heard it announced that at this day a church is being established with many in Africa, and that revelations are made at this day; and that they are receptive of the Heavenly Doctrine, especially concerning the Lord.

I was conducted through several regions in front towards the left. Afterwards I saw a great palace, and a spacious court there. A certain one spoke with me there, saying that a revelation had been promised, and that he was expecting it. And then something luminous appeared in obscurity, which was an indication that now there will be a revelation. And as I was attending, I heard that they were expecting a revelation concerning Christ, whom they call the Only Man, from whom every man is a man. And one of the angels then spoke with them, and instructed them concerning the Lord, that He is the only God. They replied that they perceived this, but not as yet that He was born a man. But when they were instructed by the angels, they understood this also, saying, that this was done for the sake of the salvation of the human race. Moreover, they knew many things respecting heaven and hell, of which Christians are ignorant. It was said that they were Africans. I was afterwards conducted thence towards the right, where I heard them saying that they had expected a revelation, and that angels were now speaking with them from the Lord, and were instructing them concerning the Lord, with the promise that they were about to receive the Heavenly Doctrine. These said that it could not be otherwise than that God, the Creator of the universe, should appear in the world, because He created men, and loves them; and that His appearing must be made even to the ocular sight in the human form.

It was afterwards shown in obscure vision how the Heavenly Doctrine would proceed in Africa; namely, towards the interior parts, even to the middle of it; and that it would then proceed towards those who were at, the sides on the Mediterranean Sea, but not to the coast; and then, after a time, would turn itself back towards Egypt. Thereupon the angels were glad, that there was now the Lord's coming anew, and that a New Church was being established, with whom they could be conjoined. That doctrine does not extend as far as to the Africans that dwell near the coasts, since the Christians come thither, who insinuate scandals, and who have a human and not a Divine idea concerning the Lord. The Africans are more receptive of the Heavenly Doctrine than others on the earth, because they freely receive the doctrine concerning the Lord, and have it as if implanted in themselves that God will altogether appear as a man. They are in the faculty of receiving the truths of faith, and especially its goods, because they are of a celestial disposition. It was told them that a prediction was made by the Lord concerning His coming, and concerning the New Church after the old one; and that His appearing is made through angels who teach.

I was conducted again to the Africans by a way running first to the north and afterwards to the west; and I saw there as it were a palace, where someone walked; and afterwards higher up, where I stopped, and heard a vast number sent forth out of the Christian heaven to those who were Africans; and those were there who in the world had lived according to their religion and had acknowledged one God under the human form. It was told them that he who has lived in good according to religion is also in the affection of truth, because the good of life desires nothing more than truth; for it desires to know how one is to live well. Thence they rejoice when they are informed; and that all such receive truths from the Lord, and are enlightened according to the quality and quantity of their good of life: this they acknowledged, and were glad. The African race can be in greater enlightenment than others on this earth, since they are such that they think more interiorly, and so receive truths and acknowledge them. Others, as the Europeans, think only exteriorly, and receive truths in the memory; nor do they see them interiorly from any intellectual light, which they do not acknowledge in matters of faith. I said there, that few Christians live according to religion, but only according to the civil laws, and live well morally for the sake of fame, honor, and gains; and that they rarely think of living according to their doctrinals; believing also that they are saved by the faith of doctrine, and not by the life: on which account they have no doctrinals of life. At this the Africans wondered exceedingly, not being willing to believe that it is so; believing that there is no man who does not live according to his religion; and if not, that he cannot but become stupid and evil, because he then does not receive anything from heaven.

All are explored after death as to what idea they have concerning God. That idea is the chief of all, because conjunction with the Lord and conjunction with heaven is according to it, and all of the love and faith of the church is hence according to it, because the Divine is the all of the church, yea, is God: hence the all of the church with a man is from his idea of God: such as that idea is, such is heaven to everyone. The Africans also differ from each other according to their idea of God. Some worship an invisible God, and some a visible one: some make of them two, and some make of them one and the same. Some have been instructed by Christians that God was born a man, and they receive this; and when they hear that they distinguish the Divine into three Persons, they go away, believing, however, that the Christians, although they say three, still think of one: for they do not comprehend what a Son born from eternity is. Some, who are the best of them, believe that God is altogether a Man. They say that those who believed that God was born a Man, formerly saw a bright star in the air. The wiser of them believe that God was born a Man in the world, and so manifested Himself.

It was said that in a certain region of Africa there is from ancient times a book which they regard as holy. It is written by correspondences in a similar manner as the Word is with us.

A certain priest, who had supposed that the idea of the Divine Human is not given with anyone, was transferred into societies of Africans, and he found that they had no other idea than that of the Divine Human.

In Abyssinia, in Africa, they have some psalms written in a style similar to that of our Word, and they sing them in their temples, and spirits are sensible of communication therefrom. In the spiritual sense they treat of one God, the Redeemer of the human race; but these things have been treated of before, where the Word is spoken of, Spiritual Experiences.

It has been granted me to speak with African spirits on various subjects, and they perceived all the truths of the church with a clear perception; and when the Word was presented to them, they understood it as to the internal spiritual sense, and carried it to their elders, who said that they have a Word with them, and that it is most holy.

They afterwards showed me the quality of those who are in Africa, which they know from the societies of that race in the spiritual world; namely, that interiorly in Africa are the best and the wise: that those that are not good are near the Mediterranean Sea, also near Egypt, and at the Cape of Good Hope. The tract where the good are, lies from Ethiopia towards the middle, into which part strangers from Europe are not admitted; and if they enter, and are not willing to perform service, they sell them to the Asiatics; and they said that at this day some speak with Africans in the world, and instruct them orally; and that their speech with them falls especially into their interior perception; and that they perceive the influx, and so receive the revelation with enlightenment; and that such speech is with their instructors, in whom they have confidence.

THE GENTILES. Concerning the lot of nations and peoples outside the church, see what has been written in Arcana Coelestia, and in the work on Heaven and Hell ; also something in the little work on The Last Judgment. That a new heaven has been formed both from Christians and from Gentiles, and also the Lord's Church on earth, see The Doctrine of the New Jerusalem.

About the time of the Last Judgment, Christians appeared there in the middle, where they were arranged at a distance from the center 2 to the circumference, and also at the various quarters according to the light of truth from the love of good. Around this middle were seen the Mohammedans arranged in like manner at the various quarters, near to the Christians according to the light of truth from good. Outside this compass were seen the Gentiles arranged according to their religion and according to life therefrom. All have similar lands divided into mountains, hills, rocks and valleys, and above them are expanses where dwell the best of them who have received from angels truths of doctrine concerning the Lord and concerning life. Beyond them appeared as it were a sea, which was the boundary. All these circuits taken together are extended not in a plane but in a globe like the earth, so that when I was conducted to the Gentiles, after passing through the Mohammedans, I descended by a declivity.

When the Last Judgment was going on, those who were in the western quarter beyond the Mohammedans, were led away towards the east. They were led, not by a circuit, but above the northern plane of the Christians, and, what I wondered at, on high, so that they were transferred by a way above the Christians, and yet did not communicate with them. And they were then allotted places around the Mohammedans at the east and also at the south. On both sides of where the Mohammedan heavens are, there appeared openings descending into the depths. Thither were cast those of them who were evil, who had worshipped idols, and had thought nothing about God, and at the same time had lived an evil life.. There is also a similar chasm on the northern side of the Mohammedan desert. Into this were cast the worst, and also many of the Roman Catholic religion who had worshipped the images of saints, and had thought nothing at all about the Lord. These latter were gathered from the northern quarter under the mountains there and were mingled with the Gentiles because they are similar. I then saw the whole northern valley even to the mountains there torn up to its foundations, and all who were there, scattered, and then there appeared in that place as it were a smokiness.

I was afterwards led beyond the Mohammedans to certain Gentiles who were in the eastern quarter, with whom it was granted to speak. They said that they were sad because the Divine does not appear to them, when yet they think of the Divine and speak about it; and, therefore, if there is a God [they had hoped] that He would send to them those who would teach them; but that they had long waited for this in vain, lamenting that perchance He had deserted them, and that thus there seemed nothing else for them but to perish. And then I heard angels speaking with them out of heaven, saying that God could not have been manifested to them because they had not been willing to believe that God was born a man in the world, or that He had taken on a Human, and that until they believe this, God cannot be manifested to them, nor can they be taught, because this is the primary thing of all revelation. They said that they did indeed believe that God is Man but that they could not comprehend that He was born Man in the world. But answer was made them, that He was not born Man like any other man, since He was not born from a human father, but from the Father Jehovah, and by a Virgin, and that thus He was unlike any other man; for a man's soul from a human father is a recipient of life, but the Lord's soul from the Father Jehovah is life itself, which gives life to all; and that the difference is as between the human and the Divine, and the finite and the infinite, or the create and the uncreate; and because He was such as to His soul, it could not be otherwise than that His body should become like His soul, after He had rejected that of the body which He had taken from the mother; and that therefore He rose as to His whole body, nor did He leave anything of it in the sepulcher, as is the case with every other man, who rises only as to his spirit, and never as to his material body. And further, it was said that the Divine itself, as it is in itself, which is infinite, could not have done otherwise than reject the finite which was from the mother, and put on the infinite from the Father, thus the Divine. They said that they had known no other than that He was like any other man born from a human father, and also that He so died, and was afterwards received by men as God, and that they now know that the Lord is not such a man as others are. After they received these things they were divided, and those who had received the faith were instructed by angels in other matters of faith and love.

I was conducted to those who in the world had known nothing about God, but who nevertheless had led a moral life amongst each other; they were said to live on a certain island. They appeared to me not like men but like apes and yet with a human face. 129-1 They so appeared because they knew nothing about God, and the Divine is in the likeness of a man. One of the Christians is set over them by the Lord. I have spoken with him, and he said that they obey him and love him; that they are modest and are engaged in employments, but that at first they could hardly comprehend the things of religion. But after some time, there was given them a nearer communication with the Christians, and they are beginning to receive something of religion, and he cherished the hope that they could be reformed, for the reason that they had lived a moral life, and are in obedience and are industrious. As to similar people elsewhere, see below. 129-2

There were likewise seen others, who had lived in an island in the West Indian seas, who had no thought at all about God, thus no religion, and who yet had lived together in a sincere and friendly way. It was told me, that at first they appear destitute of rationality, but that nevertheless, because they had contracted no false principles against religion, some of them suffer themselves to be instructed like infants, and they are perfected. It was shown that the delight of their life was to will to serve others under others. Some wealth was once given them, but they offered it to the angel who was instructing them, in order that he might receive them as his servants, that thus they might be instructed as to how they should live. It is an angelic delight to inform such spirits and to lead them to heaven.

I was once in a sweet sleep, and when I awoke I saw around me some Chinese, 131-1 and I noticed that they sat with their legs crosswise, and were talking with each other. And it was ascertained that they had been sent to me by the Lord in order that I might know of what quality many of them are. The angels said that the delightfulness of my sleep had inflowed from the fact that angels had been speaking with them about God and about the wonderful things of wisdom, and that they had been so delighted at this that they had been in the tranquillity of some celestial peace; and that evil spirits could not approach, because they were of a spiritual celestial genius.

There were with me some spirits from Tartary, 132-1 who dwelt outside the Chinese wall, saying that their country is populous; nor do they know anything about war, saying that they are without the love of reigning and that they give the government to those who say they can rule and govern, but if he cannot, he is rejected with a fine; those who do what is right and just are loved. They said that all are engaged in work, and that the lazy are cast out. They say that sometimes Christians come to them, and they marvel at their sayings that God is a Man, for they believe that all men know this. They also say that they have the commandments of the Decalogue, and that they live according to them because God so wills. They said that they have a holy book of which others do not know, and which they understand. Inquiry was made, and it was the Psalms of David. They call the Chinese their friends because they are of their nation; nor do they think of war, saying that if any strangers should come, then, unknown to them, they would all depart, taking their provisions with them. I also saw a Christian preacher with the spirits of that region. They are of a tranquil disposition.

THE LAST JUDGMENT ON THE PROTESTANTS OR REFORMED. Before the Last Judgment which was a general one, less general judgments preceded which might be called preparatory, by which those who were more exteriorly evil were cast into hells. It should be known that between the judgment effected by the Lord when He was in the world, and that of the judgment which is now effected, spirits who had outwardly lived a moral life, and had confessed God with the lips but not interiorly or in heart, had ascended upon mountains and hills and had there made for themselves, as it were, heavens, where by various arts, which are very numerous in the spiritual world, all of them unknown in our world, they had ascended on mountains; so that the world of spirits which is mediate between heaven and hell had been filled up with such heavens, and thereby the communication of the Lord and heaven with the human race had been intercepted. This also was the reason why the spiritual things of the Word and of doctrine therefrom were not disclosed until after the Last Judgment, for by the latter the world of spirits was purified and communication with man opened. If the spiritual things of the Word and of doctrine therefrom had been disclosed before, they would not have been received nor understood; and if they had been received and understood, still hell, which then prevailed, would have secretly snatched them away from men's hearts and have profaned them. Those fictitious heavens are meant in Revelation by the heaven and earth which passed away. These could pass away, but our visible heaven, which is the firmament of all things, was so created that it cannot pass away, for if this should pass away, the angelic heavens would also pass away. It would be as when the foundation is taken away from a palace, or the base from a column, whereby the house and the column would fall. For there is a connection of all things from the first to the last, from the Lord Himself to His last work which is the visible heaven and the habitable earth. The case would be similar if the human race were to perish, for thus, for a like reason, the angelic heavens would also fall to ruin.

Before the Last Judgment I often saw societies, which had made for themselves semblances of heavens, purged and also destroyed. There was one rock on which was quite a large city, where those were who were in faith separate from charity, believing as in the world, that faith alone saves, and this from mere mercy whatsoever the life may have been. They were in the lust of commanding; and therefore they stood at the sides of the rock, and in various ways infested those who were beneath. When visitation was made, and all there were found to be of such a character, I saw that the rock sank down into the depths together with the hill and the inhabitants. The like was done elsewhere. But prior to this being done, the good are separated from the evil, and the evil are in the middle; and then the middle sinks down while the borders remain; in the borders are those who are in the good of faith, that is, who are in charity.

All who have not denied God with the lips, although they have in the heart, and have led a moral life on account of the civil laws and also on account of reputation and consequent honors and gains, when they come into the other life betake themselves into societies where there are cities; and there as in the world they live well morally, from fear of punishment and of the loss of honor and gain. But when their externals are taken away from them, and they are let into their internals, they rush into infamous crimes. But when the wicked increase in number the society is then perverted; wherefore angels are then sent thither who search out the state and separate the good from the evil; and the good are either sent to the sides of the society or are taken away. Then the city with the evil sinks down into hell, to a depth according to their wickedness. Once I saw that four angels were sent to such a city, who when they came thither entered into a house; 135-1 but the criminal spirits who were there, being excited by their presence into interior malice, as takes place, rushed to the house where the angels were, shouting out to them, Did they wish to come out and commit whoredom? They wished to urge them to it, and even attempted to offer violence, but in vain; in a word, they did like what was done in Sodom. And that city was completely destroyed and its inhabitants cast into hells. The reason why they wished to lead them forth to commit whoredom, was because in that city were gathered those who in the world had accounted adulteries as allowable; also because they had been in falsities of doctrine, by reason of having regarded life as of no account; moreover, to confirm these things they had falsified the Word, and all those who falsify the Word in order to confirm evils of life and falsities of doctrine, account adulteries as allowable and are led into them.

I also saw a rock on which there had been such a city; torn up from its place and carried away to another place at a remarkable distance; it appeared carried away like a cloud. And when it came to that place I saw that it also sank down, because there was their hell. The inhabitants had been first reduced into a state of stupor.

A great number of those who are in faith separate from charity betake themselves to rocks; while those who are in the love of self betake themselves to mountains which are higher than the rocks. Hence it is that in the Word, a rock signifies faith, and a mountain love. And when, before the Last Judgment, the evil had been thus gathered together upon rocks and upon mountains, first there were suddenly felt concussions and earthquakes, by which are meant perversions of state in respect to the church, and afterwards follows the overturning, which is effected either by sinking, or by carrying away, or by casting out and thus thrusting down into hell. On the mountains and hills upon which are angels, the wisest are in the middle and the less wise at the circumferences; but on those upon which are the evil, the worst are in the middle and the better at the circumferences. The sinking in the middle appears like a vortical gyration, but in a spiral.

There was a plain somewhat more elevated than the valley. In this plain was congregated a multitude of spirits who had learned to practice evils by means of cunning, and to station themselves invisible behind others, and thus force them to think and speak what they wish them to, yea evils and falsities. They have contracted these arts by reason of their having been in the insane love of ruling over others. As it was then disclosed that their wickedness was consummated, their destruction followed. The whole of that plain was overturned; and the earth was then opened elsewhere and there rose up good spirits who had been kept concealed by the Lord in the lower earth and guarded lest they should be infested by the evil; and they succeeded in place of the former, and came in full number into possession of their land. Such things are represented by the sons of Israel to whom the land of Canaan was given after the wickedness of its nations had been consummated.

After many destructions and partial judgments had been executed, which were premonitory of the general destruction and judgment, and hordes of spirits who were impure had been cast into pools, 139-1 lakes, and chasms, that is into hells, then some came who were skilled in the art of breathing into others and exciting them to evils of interior thought. They incited some souls against the Lord and against Divine truth from Him, and from these the multitude, like one mass, began to be fermented. The tumult spread thence in every direction, as when a rebellion is started by a few persons, and yet at length stirs up a crowd. I there saw the disturbance widely spread to many rocks and mountains, even to their peaks, and thence to the sides down to the bases. Their intent was to destroy those who acknowledged and worshipped the Lord and were in Divine truths from Him. When it was noticed that the contagion had grown so wide, then was the Lord's coming for the general judgment. This coming was the Lord's influx into them through the heavens, an influx which appeared like a misty sphere spread around over those mountains and rocks; and it carried off the dwellers there, not by casting them down but by bearing them away. The Divine sphere entered into their interiors and laid them bare; and what lay concealed in their will and heart was thus made manifest. And it snatched them away and carried them down to hells according to the evils of their life. That Divine sphere was seen carried around in gyres, sometimes returning; and it also drew them out of the places where they had concealed themselves. This was done with some myriads within the space of an hour. When these things had been accomplished, the tops of the mountains receded, and the mountains themselves sank down even to the plain, and there was seen a solitude. Such things are meant in Revelation by the former heaven and the former earth which John saw pass away; for the mountains there, with the rocks and valleys, appear like the earth in our world; and the habitations upon the mountains are there called heavens. Those who were thus carried off and cast away, are they who are meant in Revelation by the dragon and his two beasts (Rev. 12-13), and by the false prophet who was cast into the lake of brimstone and fire (Rev. 19:20; 20:10).

The judgment upon the Protestants or Reformed was effected as follows: They who had led a life of charity, which may also be called a life of faith, had all been carried up into heaven long before the universal judgment; and all who in heart had denied heaven and had led an evil life had been cast by turns into hell as they came from the world. On those only was the judgment effected, who had professed religion and had acted as if from religion but only hypocritically; to these it was conceded to gather themselves together in many places in the spiritual world, and, as in the world, to simulate religion, but still they had no religion. These are they who made heavens for themselves and who are meant by the former heaven and the former earth; and by means of arts unknown in the world they are able to produce splendid things, and to persuade those who are similar that they are in heaven. Their exteriors communicated with the ultimate heaven but their interiors with the hells; and it was on account of the communication with the ultimate heaven that they were tolerated, according to the Lord's words concerning the pulling up of the tares. The angels of the ultimate heaven were first separated from them and the communication was broken; as takes place comparatively with seeds in fruits when they ripen, in that when the time comes for them to produce a new tree they separate themselves, as it were, spontaneously from the body of the fruit.

All the Protestants or Reformed of whom there was still some hope, were collected in the middle, where they were arranged according to their kingdoms in the world; for according to these were also the diversities of their dispositions or affections. But above them 141-1 and also around them were those who had read the Word and had frequented temples, but yet had made nothing of evils of life, loving themselves and the world above all things; there was an immense multitude there. Surrounding the middle region, in which were Christians who had been in the good of faith and charity, were dark caverns stretching obliquely into hells which occupied a wide space below the heaven of spirits, where were hells beneath hells. Such gulfs and chasms lay around that middle region on every side, east, west, south and north; thus the hells extended even under the circuit made by the Papists round about the Reformed. All who were interiorly evil had been disposed around the Christian middle, and from every quarter they were led down into those gulfs and cast into them. Thus, into the eastern gulf were cast those who had been collected from the east; they were such as had been in the love of self and especially in the love of ruling, nor had known anything whatever except that faith alone is saving. Into the southern gulf were cast those who had been versed in the doctrinals of faith; into the western gulf those who had been in the love of the world; and into the northern, those who had been in no understanding, but had merely heard preachings and had received no instruction afterwards.

Those at the south were led down first, then those at the west, and, lastly, those at the east. This happened at the same time that the eastern Papists were being led down beyond the northern tract.

When this had been done their dwellings were laid waste and destroyed.

Afterwards I saw an immense number of those who had lauded faith alone, and yet had possessed no faith because they had paid no attention to the evils of their life, both the learned and the unlearned, saying that they have the Word and the true doctrine, that they know the Lord, and many other things, and that, therefore, they, above others, would be saved. They were led away in a multitude, first to the west, afterwards to the south, on the other side of the waste Babylonish tract there, and even towards the east and still farther. 144-1 And they were divided; were scattered towards the north, nor were they seen anymore. And many were led back, but hither and thither; this transfer was effected in order that they might be explored as to whether they had any faith such as they had boasted of; namely, whether their faith was only a science, which is not faith; or, whether there was anything of life in it, which is faith. And it was given them to perceive that they had had no faith, but only something scientific without life.

When they were in the southern quarter near a gulf there, there came forth a multitude which had been concealed there from early times, who likewise said that they had had faith, and that they would be saved by reason of faith alone, and they had thought nothing about life. This multitude then approached them and was mingled with them.

From a certain mountain region a multitude was brought forth, who had led a moral life, not from any religion, but merely from fear of the law and of the loss of fame, honor and gain; thus without any Christian life; wherefore, so far as they could do it unknown, they perpetrated evils. Because they had not acquired to themselves any communication with heaven by means of a life from religion, they were led around to the southern and western quarters, that they might be explored as to whether they had any religion of life; and because they had none, they were rejected.

Finally came those who had been versed in the doctrinals of the church, and, in like manner, had led a moral but not a Christian life, because they had lived, not from doctrine, or the Word, but for the sake of fame, thus before men and not before God. And, being explored [it was seen] that they had nothing of conscience, because nothing of the religion of life. These were cast out of that mountain region.

All these, who were divided into the three classes, were driven so far away that they could not be seen except as a dark cloud; and they were dissipated. It was told me from heaven that they were cast down into uninhabited and desert places, and thus were separated lest they should consociate together.

The dispersion of these three classes was made to all the quarters, east, south, west, and north, whence they can never return; and this all the more, since every knowledge of religion is taken away from them. Concerning life in deserts, see elsewhere.

The angels wondered that there is so great a multitude in the Christian world who are entirely ignorant of the truth that religion is a matter of life, imagining that religion consists in thinking something or other, and that by thus thinking they absolve themselves from every obligation of life, which they have made up from this: that, by the Lord's merit, they are exempt from the yoke of the law, and that no one can do good from himself, and that if he does, it is meritorious: and yet this is so far from religion of life that it is no religion at all.

Footnotes
103-1 Tafel has, qui non volunt credere salutem per spiritum sanctum. The reading is doubtful. Acton translates it, "Who at heart wish to be saluted as the Holy Spirit."
109-1 See SE 5341-5343.
129-1 See SE 5822.

129-2 See SS 116; SE 393, 5822.

131-1 See AC 2596; SE 6067.

132-1 See SE 607; R 11; T 279; Coro 39.

135-1 See SE 4932

139-1 In the M.S. stagna is written twice; in SE 5202, lacus, "lakes," is given in place of the second stagna.

141-1 See SE 5347.

144-1 See SE 5355, 5535, 5538.

But all who have thought with themselves that evil must not be done because it is sin, and is against Divine laws, and who thus, so far as they could, have abstained from evils, all these have received something of conscience, and, in the things which were of their faith, although they were spurious, there was much life; and they were saved.

The cleansing of the middle where the Reformed were, lasted a long time; and those who were in the church without the church in themselves, or without doctrine and religion in themselves, were, by turns, cast into the gulfs surrounding the middle, and many of them into deserts. These cleansings lasted for a long time after the judgment.

I once saw many spirits, sitting around a table in a certain house, who looked like rich merchants; and still more spirits were approaching so that there were quite a number of them. In face they appeared as though upright, and they were clothed as though they were angelic spirits. But I saw that they were all cast into desert places, and into woods, thus outside the societies of the upright. The reason was stated, namely, because, in the world, they had lived, in external form like Christians and had acted well, but this solely for the purpose of acquiring a reputation for sincerity and honesty in order to make gain therefrom; and that they had not done the least thing for the sake of God or the neighbor, but all for the sake of themselves; and that, therefore, they had no communication with heaven. Hence it is that they were cast out thither, where they roam about amongst robbers, and themselves commit robbery. For when external bonds are taken away from such spirits they become robbers. They were robbers even in the world, were it not that externals, which are fears for the loss of fame and hence of gain, held them in bonds.

In the western quarter was seen a multitude whose speech sounded sincere, so that from their speech they might be thought to be, as it were, sincerities. By their speech and reasonings concerning sincerity they could induce the simple to believe that they were of such a character. But still it was found out that, within, they were like wolves, because without religion and hence without conscience. I have heard them consulting together as to how the simple might be deceived and their goods stolen away from them; some were consulting to do this, in order that they might thus obtain dominion. And then they assailed them from behind and inspired evils into them, for in this way they are able to subjugate. But their doings were seen in heaven and they were cast into a hell about the western tract of the middle region; 154-1 for they were insincerities and also wickednesses - devisers of arts with the end of gain and dominion.

Afterwards those of the Reformed were explored, as to what idea of God they had. Who had led merely a life of piety. Who had frequented temples and made themselves guilty of all sins, but had not explored themselves. Who believed that they had led a Christian life, in that they had lived well morally because of the civil laws. Who had been hypocrites.

They were explored as to what idea they had concerning God. It was found that they had thought only of God the Father, and of the Lord as like themselves; this is their belief, that the Father has compassion for the Son's sake. And they had then thought nothing concerning the Divine of the Lord. Thus, when they thought of one God they had not at the same time thought of the Lord; when yet the Father cannot be approached, since no one seeth Him but the Son alone; and that the Lord is the Way, thus that the Father is to be approached by Him; and that faith must be a faith in Him, and not in the Father. Hence they could have no determinate idea of God except as of wind, or ether, or as of nature in its leasts; and there is no Divine idea of the Lord when He is thought of as a common man. The angels complained that they were disturbed by their idea, which was communicated to them; and very many of these spirits were brought down into the quarters round about. And the places to which they came then appeared gloomy; for the true idea of God makes clearness itself. Some of them were brought into places underneath according to their life; some in order that they might be further informed. And then only those who have lived well receive a Divine idea concerning the Lord. I saw that those succeeded to their place who had been kept concealed by the Lord lest they be hurt by the contagion; these are meant in Revelation 20 by those who were slain and were delivered out of the sepulchers.

Afterwards I saw those who had led a life merely of piety, and in idleness, led away from the others. They had been continually in prayers, and not at all in truths, merely knowing that salvation is from mercy, and that sins are remitted, but knowing nothing as to what sin is. They had despised others in comparison with themselves, and had also condemned them on account of cares of the world. Most of them had placed merit in prayers. Of these also the angels made complaint, especially because they induce sadness upon them. They dwelt at the side, 157-1 wherefore they were driven away to their own places; there they retain their worship, but they are driven to work. They were brought down into the northern plain because they were in ignorance of such things as lead to heaven.

Hypocrites who have spoken well concerning God, the neighbor and the country, but in themselves have thought the contrary, were explored and cast into hell. They wished to speak well concerning the Lord's kingdom and concerning heaven, for this is then the country, but their interior thought was explored, which was for themselves alone, and against the rule of the country; wherefore, when they were let into their interiors they perpetrated criminal things. They were cast into hells, being first deprived of all that they had drawn from the Word and from doctrines by which they had deluded others.

Preachers who know something of the doctrine of their church, and, after they have been instructed in the schools, and have come into their functions, no longer care for it, nor for the Word, except that they may preach and be elevated to higher offices or may gain wealth; and thus who live in ease and are merely worldly and not Christians, these are sent into a hell in the northern quarter towards the west, far from the middle, where a dense fog is seen; and they then become stupid. 159-1

All are separated according to their life, thus according to their affections, not according to their external life, but according to their internal, for this is the life of the thought from will or affection, and no one has internal life except from religion; external life is from morality and the state, and according to its laws; wherefore moral life, unless it draw its quality from spiritual life, and thereby change its appearance, is not spiritual life with any man; consequently there is no conjunction with heaven, and they who are not conjoined with heaven are conjoined with hell; and in such case, although, in the world, they have not done evil, yet, after their departure from the world, they do evil from delight; thus their state is changed.

Concerning the Dragonists. Who are meant by the dragon, may be deduced from what has been said in the of the Apocalypse; also that by the tail of the dragon is meant faith separate from charity, which drew down the stars from heaven, that is, the knowledges of truth and good.

The dragonists were separated; many of them, when in the world, had been priests, who had confirmed themselves in faith separate from charity. They were explored in various ways, as, by the inspection, in light, of the back of the head. With those who were merely natural and hence infernal, the back of the head is filthy, hollowed out, and altogether bony. They are led down to places where they are deprived of the exteriors which have been induced on their faces by art, and the face is regarded according to the affections and the interior thoughts thence. What was human in their face is then taken away and something diabolical succeeds in its place. They are also explored by being turned to the east, and thus to the Lord; and then from the east there flows in a spiritual affection concerning the Lord. And then they instantly turn themselves back again to the west, like a spring, which recoils when it has been twisted backwards. In this way, also, angels explore newcomers to their heavenly societies.

There are also some who desire to hear truths; they believe they are saved if only they know them. But when they hear that truths are for the sake of life, and that so far as truths of life become actual, so far truths of faith also live, they then depart, feeling the utmost disgust for life, but not so for the truths which are of faith, because these they can talk about. 163-1 The truths of faith which do not live unless truths of life become actually such, may be enumerated; and it may be mentioned which are truths of faith, and which truths of life. 163-2

Everyone can see that charity consists in not stealing from anyone, either by artifice or openly; that charity consists in being wholly unwilling to commit adultery with the wife of another; that charity consists in not doing injury to the neighbor in hatred and revenge; that charity consists in not reviling another, and so forth. He who abhors these things as sins, has charity, for he loves the neighbor.

Afterwards I saw an immense number, both sent forth from the heavens and rising up from below, and also of those who had been left, who were allotted their places, mansions and habitations; in the east, those in the clear good of love and of charity; at the west, those in the obscure good of love and of charity; at the south, those in truths from good in clearness; and at the north, those in truths from obscure good; all acknowledging the Lord as the God of heaven and earth.

Many in the Christian world were also cast down who had an understanding of truth but not a will of good. In the beginning such spirits are accepted among the upright because they can speak about many things, even truths; moreover in the beginning, the understanding with them is enlightened but the will is laid to sleep. Such spirits were collected together on the mountains in the western quarter. They league themselves with the upright who are in the ultimate heaven, who do not inquire as to things of the will, but believe that those who speak intelligently are also good. But I saw such spirits, that they were altogether devoid of charity; and they secretly consociate with the evil and, first by reasonings and afterwards by arts, they infest the upright, until they are conjoined and devoted to themselves; for in this way they prevail against others. Many such were in heavens which they had made for themselves; and they interposed themselves between the Lord and man in the world, and so obstructed the way that the Divine operation could not have its force. Very many of this character are in the pride of self-intelligence from the love of self, and in the delight of domineering. I once saw such spirits in a somewhat high mountain in the western quarter toward the north, and everywhere round about on the sides of the mountain; and they persuaded themselves and others that one is in heaven from mere intellectual light and not at the same time from heavenly heat; they are most dangerous. I saw them cast down from the mountain and from the sides of the mountain, and a gulf underneath opened itself and swallowed them up, 166-1 and they sank deep down and were let into darkness. For they then received falsities in place of truths, and turned themselves to things contrary. Such is the understanding which is led by an evil will. The evil who had conjoined themselves with them, because they no longer had the power of resistance, were cast down into their various hells, some into hells under the mountains, others into hells under the plains. 166-2

Those who were in faith separate rose up in insurrection, exciting a rebellion well-nigh universal. Their dogma and their learned leaders rose up against those who acknowledged the Lord and a life of love from Him. They stirred up all, except those who were in the eastern quarter, these were guarded by the Lord, even to certain Mohammedans who were in the northern quarter. They sent forth companies of fifty to many places, in order that they might stir up those who were there; 167-1 and those who remained and directed were divided into companies of ten. Their purpose was to destroy all those who acknowledged the Lord alone, and works together with faith as being saving. Almost all of them were without religion, and hence without conscience. But when they set out to do this, and were in the endeavor to destroy others that were evil, a force flowed down from on high, or from heaven, by which they were cast down to the hells, to a number exceeding many thousands. They also conjoined themselves with Papists and with monks who in the world had proclaimed themselves Christs and had thought nothing of the Lord's Divinity. When the whole crew had been cast down, the leaders were taken; and they became black as devils, both within and without; and they became so monstrous that they would be scarcely recognized as men. For man is such as he is as to life; he who is black as to life, afterwards becomes black even from head to heel. It was found that they had not rebelled from zeal on account of the doctrine of faith alone, but from the delight of ruling and of doing evil for the sake thereof. This was the combat of Michael with the Dragon; for all such who have insinuated themselves into heaven are drawn forth thence and cast down. They are Michael who worship the Lord and [who make] works conjoined with faith saving; for since the one is not given without the other, therefore they save conjointly.

The combat of the Dragon with Michael was afterwards as follows, for it lasted some days: A hand was seen stretched out over the heavens by the Lord. In the western quarter towards the west 168-1 there appeared as it were a great back raised above the middle towards heaven; angels in immense number were seen there. In that entrance were the dragonists; and they spoke with them concerning the Lord and concerning the goods of charity and thence of faith. All then turned towards them to hear what they would say. And the dragonists were forced into the thoughts concerning the Lord and concerning faith alone which they had in the world; and then most of them had no Divine idea of the Lord, nor any idea of charity and works. The angels answered them wisely on this matter, but in vain. They said, moreover, that all the angels in the heavens do not perceive the matter thus; but it was in vain. 168-2 And at last, after the combat, when the dragonists were only willing to give further response outside of the matter or the truth, but could not, they were adjudged to be cast down from every place where such spirits were. But when they said they would resist, the Lord was seen descending from the sun in a bright cloud, and He gave judgment that all who were found to be such should be separated and alienated. And then they were cast down successively and by turns according to the connection of the societies of heaven; towards the western quarter an immense number, and a thousand then appeared as one. The grievous collision of truth and falsity which pertained to temptation was felt within me. The whole western quarter was full of such spirits who had been cast down from the heavens; and then the earth was seen to open, and they were cast down and were covered over with a dense cloud. They were all such as would never have abstained from thinking and willing evils but only from doing them by reason of fear. This happened in 1757 on the 11th day of April. 168-3 From the southern quarter to the western the dragonists were seen in a curved line under the figure of a tail; at the south, there, were those who had been skilled in the degrees of justification and had confirmed these with themselves.

The Lord's heaven was first inherited by such as had acknowledged Him and had lived well, who had had heaven in themselves; afterwards, succeeded those who wished merely to have heaven outside themselves. To these latter it was also granted to make heavens for themselves, which they called heaven when they saw the magnificent things, such as palaces, porticos, paradises, and many serviceable things. But, since their internals were not in correspondence, such things disappeared; and then by phantasies and the abuses of correspondences and by many arts, they provided for themselves things similar. This did not last long, however, for they placed everything in delicacies and in bodily pleasures, and thus they became wholly external such as they had been in the world; and then came the judgment, after which followed continual purifications of the societies from such spirits.

Many of those who are in faith alone, because they have no conjunction with heaven but all conjunction with hell, are in the love of ruling. They are explored in the following way: From the societies of heaven they look down to the places beneath; and where they see spirits, whether many or few, walking about there, they rule their thoughts, infest them in various ways, and by phantasies cause many things to appear to them to which they are led; their joy is to precipitate them into hells. They are of such a character that they do not want to be led but to lead; this is their delight; wherefore they cannot be led by the Lord, for the Lord leads through the affection of use, and this is not their affection. With them use is to domineer, and, therefore, they successively deny the Lord, and rely upon arts, which are many, by which they have dominion. They put their trust in their own prudence, and ascribe nothing to the Divine Providence and when the reins are loosened, they rush finally into such a state that they think there is no God. And yet inseated in them is the purpose of domineering over heaven and to be there in place of God. This is inseated in the love of ruling for the sake of self. I once saw that a certain spirit in a small society was permitted to set in order those who were there. He set them in order as a spider sets its webs, placing himself in the middle and making paths in every direction, with the command that all should look to him; but that society was swallowed up by the hells which were below. All who are of such a character wish to be in the heavens; and they climb up into high places, where they believe that the exercising of dominion is the delight of life, but use is this; but when they have been explored they are cast down. They are wanderers; they direct their course from one society to another, often seeking to obtain office.

They are distinguished according to their ideas of the Divine, as They who have an idea concerning the union with the Father. They who have an idea solely of the Lord's Human and nothing of the Divine, although they had known of it. They who have acknowledged three Persons and have not made them one God by essence; these are specially distinguished. They who have an idea solely of the Father; these are without a God. They who have not believed in the Lord from eternity. 171-1

All those are preserved who in the world had acknowledged the Divine of the Lord and had shunned evils as sins, especially those who had acknowledged the Divine Human, and had approached Him. But the rest who had thought of the Lord as of a common man, are cast back among the Socinians and Arians who, at first, are under the heavens nearest above the hells, and afterwards are in the hells.

They who were in faith alone persecuted me. They brought persecution upon me 173-1 by bringing me into a state like that in which they themselves were by means of a like respiration and a like pulse; thus also into like thought and affection. And, in respect to God and salvation, I was in an obscure cloudiness as though immersed in water; and it was perceived that I had no communication 173-2 with heaven; and it was said that they have a similar communication.

Many of those who are in faith alone and had committed nothing of truth and good to life, for the reason that they had rejected all moral life from a spiritual origin, saying that it effects nothing, and that evils do not condemn, and that the Lord had fulfilled the Law for them, and had taken away damnation, and that of themselves they cannot do good still less fulfill the Law, many of these become rebels and put forth various scandals against the Lord, as is the case with all who have not lived their religion, even if in the world they had not thought wickedly concerning the Lord. They were explored and it was found that they had committed nothing of truth and good to life, and that they

merely knew something from the Word which was like any other scientific
matter in which there is nothing vital. And they then appeared without
clothing, for clothing signifies the truths of life; and then they understand
nothing at all, even as to what was right and just. It was said to them that they
had lived without religion, and they were cast into the southern gulf, and were
thus carried away.

Some of this character were let out of hells in order that they might be
transferred to another hell. And it was then permitted them to act according to
their will. Then they at once desired to force their way up to higher places by
means of phantasies, and they were in the endeavor to do evil. It was recalled
to their memory that, in hell, they had said to each other, that if it were allowed
them to go out, they would be just as wise as others. Certain ones then spoke
with them, saying something of intelligence in which was the light of truth; and
when they heard them they were seized with such anguish that they fled away.
This was done several times in order that it might be confirmed that such
spirits, even when the state is changed, do not sustain the light of truth, thus
of intelligence. They said that they were doing them harm, but answer was
made that with each other they said otherwise. Hence it was made clear that
they who are in hell can never live in the light of heaven, thus in heaven; and
least of all in the heat of heaven, which is love.

After the judgment, all societies were disposed according to nations, in an
admirable order. The order was according to affections in the heavens, and
according to cupidities in the hells. They are then straightway purified by
means of communications with the evil, and thence as it were by a
fermentation; and then the alien are cast down like things heterogeneous.
Sometimes the purification is effected by the society becoming like one man;
they who are in the man remain, they who are outside the man are rejected.
After the judgment, it is not permitted to thus ascend into heaven and be cast
down thence, but each one is determined in such direction that he may go the
way that leads to his society.

Afterwards societies were formed most distinctly according to all the genera
and species of the affections of good and of truth; and also corresponding
infernal societies. All spirits, after they have been vastated, are now led along
by designated ways tending to the interior societies which correspond and are
analogous to their life; nor are they allowed as before to turn aside in any other
direction, or to stay in other places, still less to form for themselves societies and
as it were heavens, according to life in externals. It is perhaps believed in the
world, that man is saved and comes into heavenly societies according to his
thoughts which are of the understanding of truth; but no one is saved according
to these, but according to affections and thoughts thence, thus according to the
good of the will and thence the truth of the understanding. For man is man
from his will and his understanding thence, and not from the truth of the
understanding separate from the good of the will; the understanding merely
teaches how man must will and act. Many are led along the designated ways
with difficulty, for they wish to go to the sides where they are sensible of the
presence of the good both below and above, to whom they are eager to do evil;
for all ways are such as are the societies above and below them.

The arranging of the Reformed after the judgment lasted a long time, for the reason that the Word is with them and the Lord is known, and they are therefore in the middle; and the greatest light is there, which passes from that middle to the peripheries where are also the Gentiles. On this account the arranging of the Reformed lasted a long time.

All those are retained in the heavens who have had the delight of some use, or of some function for the sake of use, whether it be the delight of business from sincerity, or of some study, provided only there be the delight of use and the acknowledgment of God. These can be held in order by the Lord, because the Lord inflows into uses. But they who have led a life of idleness, merely in social companies, or in offices solely for their own glory, cannot be ruled by the Lord; and because they are not members of the society, considered as a man, they are rejected. There is an application to the function of the blood.

HE-GOATS; THEY ARE THOSE WHO ARE IN FAITH SEPARATE FROM CHARITY. Speech was held with some in regard to the he-goat mentioned in Daniel and to its combat with the ram; and also in regard to the judgment on the goats and sheep mentioned in Matthew. And beneath me there then appeared a he-goat with great horns which was seen to infest the sheep and to treat them badly with its horns, and also to toss them hither and thither. And inquiry was made as to what this was, and it was said that this was the appearance of those who are in faith separate from charity, and of their combat with those who have been in the life of charity. And it was said that before their own eyes they do not look like this but like men sharply disputing with each other; and that he who seemed like a he-goats, was one who was in faith separate, while they who seemed like sheep were those who were in the life of charity. For sometimes, and especially at a distance, spirits appear according to their affections, inclinations, and their principles therefrom. For example, when anyone is thinking from the understanding, he appears as though sitting on a horse, and some appear in other ways. Hence it was made evident that by the horned he-goat in Daniel, and by the he-goats in Matthew, none others are meant. It is supposed that all the evil are meant by the he-goats, but no others of them are meant than those who have lived wickedly and have nevertheless confessed faith alone. [Marginal Note:]   After the Last Judgment was accomplished many were seen who had been scattered among others at the back in the west; at a distance they appeared like he-goats, and some like dragons; who because they wished to seduce the upright were removed thence and driven into deserts where there was scarcely a shrub.

In like manner afterwards, those who were in faith separate, appeared as he-goats, and those who were in the life of charity as sheep, and their argumentations and wranglings, as combats.

. THE DRAGON. By "the dragon" (Revelation 12), and by his "two beasts" (Chap. 13), no others are meant than those who are in faith separated from charity both in doctrine and in life, by "the dragon," all those who have confirmed themselves in that faith, and by the beast from the sea, they who have confirmed those principles by means of reasonings from the natural man, and by "the beast from the earth," who is afterwards meant by "the false prophet," are meant confirmations from the Word in favor of that faith. That such are meant by "the dragon and his two beasts," may be clearly seen from each particular there written about them, understood in the spiritual sense;

which can be seen to the life if the things written on Revelation should be given to the public, for they are all confirmed from heaven; also that by "the tail of the dragon," is meant the confirmation of that faith by means of the degrees of justification which are treated of in [Spiritual Experiences.

The Apocalypse treats of the two religious systems in the Christian world, that with the Reformed and that with the Papists, for the whole of Christianity is from these two, since they are the ruling systems. The religious system with the Reformed is a system of faith alone, which has devastated the church; and that with the Papists deals with the Lord's vicarious authority over the church, thus over the souls of men, and also over heaven, that resides with the popes and the primates and subordinate officials of the church. It is these two ruling systems of religion which [have been rejected] by the Last Judgment, concerning which we will treat later.

That they who are in faith separate are meant by "the dragon and his beasts." That by "the dragon" are meant those who are in faith separate was made evident from the following circumstances: It is related that "the dragon stood by the woman about to bring forth, that he might devour her ;" and that, by "the son, which the woman was about to bring forth," is meant the doctrine concerning the Lord and concerning the life of charity, was made evident from this, that when that doctrine was being written many of those who are in faith alone were present, and in such fury, that I could scarcely have written had I not been guarded by the Lord by means of angels; and it appeared as though they wished to rend it and tear it to pieces. By "the woman" there, is meant the New Church which is the New Jerusalem, and by her son, the doctrine concerning the Lord and concerning the life of charity; and by "the dragon," are meant those who are in faith separate, because such then was their nature, and because they were about to do what is described afterwards, by persecuting the woman, and casting forth water like a flood, that he might swallow her up; by "water like a flood," falsities are signified.

There was a certain preacher who was in faith alone; he appeared to others altogether like a dragon, and he also seemed to hover around a woman about to bring forth, eager to devour her child; and yet, seen near at hand, he was standing near those who defended the life of charity and the Lord. He was a preacher at The Hague.

Of those who are in faith separate there are some who correspond to the head of the dragon, some who correspond to his body, and some who correspond to his tail. The latter are they who are in the conceit of those principles, for the tail is the continuation of the spinal cord, and this again of the brain. There are some who correspond to the poison.

Concerning the back and hinder part seen like the tail of a dragon, see above 134-179]. [On the Reformed], towards the end of the chapter.

Moreover at the left was seen a hillside upon which ascended many of those who were in faith alone; and on the summit there, they have some bearded old man who had been bearded in the world, and sometimes of lowly condition. This man persuades them that he is God the Father. It is a rock and rocky places are around about it. And when they do not wish to be seen they betake themselves behind the mountain. These are they who have laid snares for all who do not believe like themselves, believing that this is allowable. The life of charity they make of no account. By their interiors they make one with the hells. They who appeared round about the bottom of the mountain were seen like an immense dragon stretching itself towards the places below; and its tail was seen elevated and extended from the mountain to the lowest parts thereof.

FAITH ALONE. The interior sphere of spirits was perceived to be completely filled with affections, which are ends, of becoming great, of growing rich and of being wise for the sake of glory, and little, if at all, on account of the common good.

When, from the Lord, I was in the faith of the knowledges of truth it was found that evil spirits were powerless to refute them or even to reason about them as when I was in the knowledges that the Lord rules the universe, that the Lord alone is life, and that the proprium of man is nothing but evil, and others of a like kind. Evil spirits hearing these, although they did not believe them yet could not contradict, for truth is averse to it, because the intellectual does not admit any thinking against it. From this it was made clear that those who are in the simple faith of truth resist evils. I also saw some, who were in truths, who passed through many hells and all the infernals retreated, nor could they approach, still less do any evil. But he who believes in the faith set forth in the church at this day, cannot do this; the infernals are in no way troubled at their approach, because truth from the Lord is not in that faith.

Concerning certain spirits who have no spiritual life because they are in ignorance of truth; and that life is inspired into them by the Lord through angels. I once felt a somewhat intense cold from the soles of the feet up to the knee; it became evident that there were cold spirits. It was told me that they were those who in the world had lived in absolute ignorance of God. After they had been elevated I heard them talking, and I could perceive scarcely anything vital in their speech. They spoke as though they were making inanimate statues speak, and I despaired of any life long remaining in them. They were like automatons or sounding sculptures. But presently I heard that they had been let into a species of activity appearing like a species of gyration. Angels were caring for them by infusing life into them, which they did with such solicitude and devotion, that it can scarcely be described, nor did they suffer themselves to be wearied. In the meantime they waved them, as is said in the Word of the things sacrificed, that they were waved by the Levites, the reason being, that they might receive spiritual life. When this had been done for some little time, they began to be vivified, and to be no longer of such a nature as before; thus they began to speak something in consociation, saying that they were in heaven. The work was continued by the Lord through angels during the whole night, and after this they became such as to be capable of being insinuated or inserted into some companies in which they were afterwards perfected. For they were receptive of life because they had nothing repugnant thereto, as have those who confirm themselves in falsities against truths. The manner in which life was successively insinuated into them was represented by colors, the first of life by a marble color increasing in whiteness, the second by a growing azure color in which was the white, and the third by patches of bright clouds rising up. Their quality was afterwards shown me by a blowing from them on my face, and also into the anterior region of the breast. It was somewhat cold but verging to heat. This was from the Lord alone by means of angels. They may be said to be resuscitated from no life into some life.

There was one who held it as a principle that faith alone saves; it was said to him that faith is like science and knowledge which should be for the sake of use and good, and that otherwise it is nothing but a science; also that he is insane who believes that science alone saves, when yet all science and knowledge has good as an end.

He who has fought against evils, and, from the Lord, has come into the love of good and truth, is in the knowledges of truth and good as it were from himself; he sees them in himself, and they are inscribed on his heart, as is said in Isaiah and Joel. The rational is then enlightened. But prior to this he does not know them, except from the memory alone, in which case he does not see them except externally, and if they are not seen internally they are dry and transitory. This is the life in truths; for all the things of truth are inscribed on the love, just as, with every animal, all things which are for use are inscribed on the affection, as in the case of bees, birds, and other animals; so also are they inscribed on man if he is in the genuine love of truth and good. It is from this that the angels have their wisdom.

I was led through societies or mansions of heaven, and I spoke with many. And when I came to mansions of the third heaven, where are the celestial, I wished to speak with them about the knowledges which are called knowledges of faith and which in themselves are truths. I marveled that they did not wish to make any response to these things. They said that they see all things in themselves from the love in which they are, which was love to the Lord and mutual love, saying that the truths of their faith were inscribed on their life, and that therefore they see them from the light of truth which is from the Lord, and this because in good is contained all truth. They also said, What are knowledges except for the sake of uses? and uses are goods, and goods are of love. It was told me that they are of this nature because, in the world, they had applied all the truths they had heard to their life. All their love and all their faith consists in deeds.

Those who are in faith alone believe in instantaneous salvation and pure mercy; and therefore they implore mercy alone and believe that they are instantly saved the moment they receive faith, even though it be in the last hour of death. They also believe that the remission of all sins consists in the wiping away of all evils. They have no comprehension of remission by means of repentance of life, but only of remission by means of faith arising from thinking such things as they call of their faith; thus they are ignorant of all the means of salvation. It was shown them that such things are a phantasy; and this phantasy was represented as being interiorly full of poisonous serpents. The nature of the phantasy was shown in a ludicrous manner, namely, that they think and also wish to void those serpents through their posteriors.

When they think from their doctrine about faith alone, and are opposed by the statement, in The Epistle of James, that men should show their faith by works, there appears as it were a knife flying forth to slay those who perceive this to be the case. And from one side comes forth an idea of Luther, and from the other, whither the knife flies, an idea of James, although Luther and James themselves are not there. The reason is, because, Luther excluded the Epistle of James.

Below, at the left, are those who from doctrine have confirmed themselves in regard to faith alone, but yet have lived a life of charity from the principle that faith produces the works of charity. These, because they have lived well, are accepted and have conjunction with heaven. Still it is not a direct conjunction, and this for the reason that they hold it as a principle that it is faith that produces the works of charity, when yet faith is of the thought, and thought produces nothing; it only teaches what should be done, and if a man does what it teaches, then it is not from any faith; for knowledges of truth do not become knowledges of faith until man has done them. It is like one who believes that the sight operates into the hands to enable a man to work, or into the feet to enable him to walk and not stumble, when yet the sight does not operate in this way, but it teaches and brings things to view. That this is an inversion was shown by it being given to a certain spirit to walk on a road and to then believe that it was the understanding that was leading him. He then went from the east to the west or from the south to the north, thus from truths to falsities, and into obscurity. But his state was changed [so that he believed] that the will or love was leading him; he then walked from the west to the east and from the north to the south, thus into good and into truth in light. It was told them that with those who have had this belief the state is successively inverted, and that then they begin to be regenerated and come into the angelic life.

They who, from doctrine, are in the principle that faith alone saves, and yet have led a good life, constitute certain societies in which they are in the middle, while at the circumferences are those who are not of such a quality, and lastly those who are evil, so that they are surrounded by the evil. It was told them that they still dwell among the evil.

It was made known by living experience that those who have been in faith alone and have led a moral life, had made heavens for themselves, where they seemed to themselves to have been in light; but it was shown that it is a wintry light, for when angels looked thither, in place of light there appeared a thick darkness. Those who go there, and are at the same time in charity, feel a pain in the breast, the stomach and the knees.

Concerning those who are continually wrangling about truths. There are hells where they do nothing else but wrangle about truths. One of them was under the groins. In that hell were those who believe that they know everything and that nothing is hidden from them, when yet they do not know anything, except that their faith is the all of the church with men. There are those there who, by reason of their belief that they know all things, think that they alone are entitled to talk; they despise the laity. They are continually saying that this is the truth itself, and that it cannot be contradicted. I have there heard perpetual contradictions and quarrels which went so far that they wished to attack their opponents with their fists, but they are held back by others. They appear in that place as if they were tearing garments; and from the place is heard as it were the gnashing of teeth. Thus do they go forward and back and thus do they wrangle, not at all for the sake of truth but for the sake of themselves from the pride of their own intelligence and from the itch of domineering. They are removed from others, because they disturb all tranquillity of mind and take away the freedom of thinking from the Word, inducing their own opinions as though they were from the Divine and infesting all who do not receive. At this day there are many such consociations drawn from the Christian world, because there they have divided the church on questions of opinion concerning what is to be believed, and the good of life they not only reject, but they also say that they know not what it is unless it be to give to the poor and to hear preachings.

Footnotes
154-1 See SE 5398.
157-1 See SE 5392.
159-1 See SE 5514.
163-1 See SE 5540, 5541.
163-2 Tafel has, delati, possibly it is detecti. See SE 5696, 5698.
166-1 See SE 5698.
166-2 See SE 5699.
167-1 See SE 5731 1/2, 5758.
168-1 The M.S. has, ocvcidentem, "west." In SE 5742 it is septentrionalem, "north."
168-2 See SE 5722.
168-3 See SE 5746.
171-1 See SE 5821.
173-1 Tafel has, eamque mihi intulerunt; the MS., me persecuti mihi intulerunt. In SE 5827 it is, Se congregarunt, et violentiam inferebant, "They gathered themselves together, and inflicted violence."
173-2 See SE 5827.

Those who have said that they had faith have been seen many times; and when they are explored it is found that they had no other faith than that which was spoken of above. This they call the only saving faith, and also spiritual faith, and yet they have not lived any Christian life by shunning evil because it is sin. They were sent into places where faith was constituted of truths which had their essence from the good of life, and their communication was granted them to discover whether they had faith. And, from the perception then given them, they themselves openly confessed that they had nothing of faith, it was mere knowledge like any other mere knowledge of the world, and that they had not known what faith was; also that faith was truth, and that, unless truths are from good; they are not truths, but are only articulated expressions of sound.

Very many of those who are in faith alone and in no life of charity are sensual. For evils of life, which they neither see in themselves nor have endeavored to see, occupy their voluntary and make it; and, as a man is in respect to his voluntary such he is as to his interiors. Therefore these interiors are shut up, and all things which are of the church and heaven are below or without, thus merely in the memory where they reside as historical faith or as science. This is the reason why, when men hear something of the truths concerning the Lord, the Word, eternal life, heaven, the state of the angels and the state of men after death, the things they hear are received as matters of the memory; but as soon as they think about them, as to whether they are so, then the sensual corporeal judges and makes its own conclusion. The conclusion reached is that what has been heard cannot be true, and this because what is previously in the memory from doctrine must be believed; as, that there are three Persons of the Divinity, that the Human of the Lord is not Divine, that angels, because they are spirits, are like winds, and so likewise man after death. The reason is because it is the sensual that makes the conclusion, and [in that] light from heaven which enlightens cannot be received, the interiors being closed to the transflux of that light. Investigate for yourself as to whether this is not the case, whenever any such truth is laid under direct examination, and inquiry is made as to whether it is so. The sensual man is such that he comprehends fallacies and believes in appearances and speaks truths, but the truths themselves, which are of the light of heaven, he rejects. This is the effect of faith alone, and therefore they cannot be led on into any understanding of truth.

It was said by angels that there can be no such thing as faith alone. Spirits who, in the world, had been in faith alone, being indignant at this, came running up from every direction to where the angelic spirits were, and inquired, "Is there no such a thing as faith alone?" In this manner they ran to ten or fifteen places, and everywhere received the answer, that there is no such thing, because faith without love is mere knowledge, and their faith the mere knowledge of falsity; and if they wish to call mere knowledge faith, because they have persuaded themselves in it, although they do not understand whether it is so, [their belief] is nothing but persuasion because it is so said, and is scarcely different from the belief that corpses and bones and men's graves are holy, when yet they are stercoraceous and signify damnation and hell. When they heard this they ran on and inquired what love was, whether it was not faith alone. Angelic spirits thought them insane, and still more when they said that works were faith, which is as if they had said that thinking was doing. They ran on still further and said, "Is not faith thus a nonentity?" They received the answer that faith separate from charity is a nonentity, because faith is called faith from charity which is its soul; and faith separate from charity is just such an entity as is the body without the soul.

I have heard many of the learned reasoning about various matters of their faith, things which they had held from birth, thence as truths of their religion. Their reasoning was sharp and vehement and each one was refuting the other. There were angels who were listening and they said that with not a single one of them did they perceive any affection of truth, nor therefore any sight of truth, and thus no delight of mind arising from any truth. They wondered that these spirits were able to confirm falsities; and they said that it was merely the delight of reasoning springing from pride, and that thus they cannot progress into any wisdom, for they are at a standstill. But those who are in the affection of truth are ever progressing from truth to truths, and this continually until at last they come to wisdom and thus to angelic happiness. They said that as soon as they hear such reasoners, they turn themselves away and have no wish to join company with them because they see nothing. Of such quality are very many of those who have confirmed themselves in faith separate, not only in doctrine but also in life; for they think to themselves, "What need have I to know what evil is since this does not condemn? or what good is since this does not save? Only let me think, from that faith, that the Lord has fulfilled for me all things of the law and that His merit will be imputed to me."

It was disclosed by angels of heaven that those who are in faith alone have no conscience, yea, that they do not know what conscience is; and he who has no conscience has no religion. The reason is, because they make goods of life of no account, and they who make these of no account can by no means have conscience, and hence cannot know what it is; for conscience is a grief of the mind that one has done contrary to the Divine precepts and that one has thought against them. Grief of conscience arises from this, that they see themselves as it were in damnation.

They who believe that man is saved by charity and not by faith alone, if they do not live the life of charity, differ little from the others. For to say charity or to say faith, and not to do them, are both equally of the thought, in which there is nothing of life because nothing of the will. Such spirits inflict pain in the breast and in the right shoulder blade.

How greatly the principles of falsity injure the mind and turn it away from deeds, may appear from many examples. Thus he who believes that works contribute nothing to salvation turns his mind away from doing goods. He who believes adulteries are allowable turns his mind away from chaste conjugial love, thus from chastity, yea from purity of faith; for purity of faith is wholly discordant with adulteries. He who believes that nature operates all things, and that God operates only in a universal way, trusts in his own prudence, and does nothing of good except from himself. Wherefore principles of falsity inflow into the life; for the will does not act contrary to the principles that have been received, but with them.

I have spoken with Melancthon about faith alone, to the effect that he could see from reason alone, that faith alone is not saving because every man is his own good and his own evil; and that every spirit is a form and image of his own good and his own evil; and this not only as to his face but also as to his whole body. For according to the quality of a spirit's affection such he is in respect to his mind, and at the same time in respect to his body. This may be manifestly known from the fact that when anyone speaks contrary to the affection of any spirit or angel, he immediately changes his countenance, yea, becomes invisible and disappears. And, therefore, because faith alone is merely of the thought and not of the will, and thus only of the memory and not of the life, it follows that it is as yet outside the man and not within him. Wherefore, since a spirit is a complete spirit in the degree that he is his own good or his own evil, and since faith separate from good is not within the man, it follows that it is merely like a skin, and that men of faith separate are not men except as to the skin; and thus that they are to be called cutaneous.

The truth is, that he who confirms faith alone with himself both in doctrine and in life cannot be reformed, and thus cannot be saved; that is, he who, while in the world, has thought, "Since I am justified by faith nothing of evil will condemn me, because it is not imputed, and nothing of good will save me;" and has thus cast out of his thought all reflection upon the evil and the good of life with himself; and if he apperceives any evil or good he is not concerned about it as being a matter of no importance in respect to salvation. Such are spirits who cannot be reformed, for they think like things after death.

That the Lord is love; that hence the whole heaven is arranged according to the genera and species of love, and thus according to its varieties; that in like manner every society of heaven, and every spirit and angel; that it is similar in a spirit and angel in whom heaven is, in that all things in them are disposed from love and, according to it in their understanding, yea, their whole body. How then can there be such a thing as faith alone, since faith is according to love?

There was a certain Englishman, who had written learnedly and skillfully about faith and charity, and this from considerable ingenuity. But he had come to the conclusion that faith produces charity, and that when man is justified by faith he is in the endeavor to do good, and that this is the effect of faith; thus that faith first leads to charity and afterwards in charity. It was told him by angels that it so appears to man, and yet that it is not so; and, because it so appears, that this is the way of reformation, for thus man learns many things which are of faith, believing that in this way he is saved; but when man is not regenerated the order is inverted. And, moreover, that if he should make inquiry he would never find that faith produced charity, but that faith was produced by charity. And, therefore, because he was gifted with much ingenuity, he thought out many reasons for confirming the idea that it is faith that produces; and it was permitted him to produce these reasons, and to show whether the case was so. Wherefore in his meditation he was left to follow out each reason; but when he came to the end of his production there always appeared, as it were, an obstruction to the way which he was unable to penetrate so as to arrive at charity. Therefore, abandoning this reason, he acted in a similar manner with another reason, and so on with a hundred. In this way he went on in his ingenious meditation every day for an entire year, and not once did he see a conjunction on the part of faith. Wherefore he afterwards confessed that the thing was impossible, and that the fact that some said they had felt it with themselves was due either to their having thought of charity outside of faith, or to other causes, etc., etc., which arose from the fact that the things which are of faith have taught them, for the truths of faith teach and man acts according to them, and that from a principle either adopted or heard, they have attributed it to faith. Moreover, after a man has done charity, faith is then living, and then, in the single things, charity and faith work together, and it can hardly be seen which is prior and which posterior. The truths of faith which are of the thought and understanding are prior-but still truths do not live and become truths of faith or saving until man lives according to them.

I read before Englishmen their exhortation used before the Holy Supper , how they should act that their sins may be forgiven, and in which there is no mention of faith; and I said this is true religion itself. Certain preachers who were in favor of faith alone, hearing this, said that when reading that exhortation in their churches they had fully believed it to be the way of salvation, but when thinking from their doctrine of faith alone they had thought differently. The English were praised for that exhortation, and many of them believed that it belonged to their doctrine; but more of them said that this was for the common people, faith alone being for the learned. They were asked whether they wished to thus invite the curse expressed in the words, that unless they do this Satan would enter into them as he entered into Judas. They then went away and spoke about the matter among themselves.

I once saw some leaders of the English, among whom were also one or two bishops, who fought for faith alone as for their altars and hearths. And from the ideas of their thought concerning faith alone and justification thereby they formed an image, that it might represent that faith. In the spiritual world this can be done skillfully and easily. They there made their images by means of ideas, and these images also became visible, for appearances are merely from their ideas. Into their image they fitted all things of their faith. But when it was finished it appeared in the sight of the angels as an enormous monster, and as though it would frighten them away. This was in the light of heaven; but before their own eyes it assumed a different appearance, as monstrous things are wont to do, when seen in darkness and from phantasy. They gloried in it at first, but afterwards they became ashamed.

The English said that faith produces charity as a tree produces fruit. But it was shown them that by a tree there is not meant faith but man, and by the branches and leaves are meant the truths of faith, and by the fruits the goods of love; also that natural affection or natural good, which is of the love of self and the world, cannot be conjoined to a faith which is spiritual; if it is conjoined, the result is an adultery; and that spiritual good is not possible except by means of the good of life, which is the good treated of.

An argument on which they lay stress is, that man cannot do good which is good of himself. This is true, but still unless man be in good as from himself it is not appropriated to him, and so he is not conjoined to the Lord. In order for conjunction there must be something reciprocal, and thus a covenant, which is, If you do that I will do this. And, therefore, that man may do it as if of himself freedom is given him, and this freedom is freedom to think, to will, and to do; reason is given him that he may see what salvation is; will is given, and choice and election; and he is commanded to act. All these are given in order that he may act as if of himself, and yet it is not from him but from the Lord. If he did not act of himself he would be an automaton, and all influx would pass through him. The Lord is continually with man pressing and urging him that he may act, and that, for the sake of appropriation and conjunction, it may appear no otherwise than that he acts of himself. A thousand passages can be adduced showing that man is condemned if he does evil and rewarded if he does good; those where doing and works are mentioned might be brought forward.

Many were explored who at the last hour when they had received the Sacrament believed they would be saved by that faith. They said they had believed with trust and confidence; yet it was the life of evil that remained and not the faith. They were told to hold their breath and, at the same time, retain that faith, but still, as soon as they breathed, the delight of evil, from which was their life, returned; and they were cast into hell.

After the judgment those who had been scattered amongst others round about were collected together. And when they had been collected, there came into their mind a cunning of seducing the upright [by teaching them] that faith alone is saving. Wherefore the latter complained about them to the Lord. And then I saw them receding more and more, even till they came to the bounds of the Christian world; there, at the back, were deserts, and I saw a great part of them driven thither. Afterwards it was granted me to see the nature of this desert. There were vile huts and hovels wherein they dwelt almost solitary, with some harlot, and round about them it was stony, with great heaps of rocks between which were a few ways. Nor does one dare to approach another. They all fear each other lest they do evil, nor do they believe even when they stand outside and invite them in. A piece of bread with water is given them daily; some send them something eatable. I saw no shrub, still less any tree; but sandy and rocky places.

Many of them said they were desirous of being instructed and thus of rejecting that faith, but in vain; 218-1 the inrooted faith clung to them because it had been the principle of their life. What is marvelous, the learned of that religion regard justification by faith alone as such a Divine mystery, that touching it is like touching the pupil of the eye; saying that they have bound themselves to it by oath. But it was shown them that in the Revelation it is described by the beast from the sea [Rev. 13:1-10], and in Daniel by the little horn which waxed great towards all the quarters, and cast down from heaven the host thereof [Dan. 8:9-10]. But when they hear this confirmed from heaven, where correspondences are perceived, they still worship justification as their idol. The justification that is meant is justification by faith separate from charity. I also spoke much about the endeavor to do good which follows justification, asking them whether this endeavor is anything of the will on man's part. They said that it was: others said that it was not, but was to be carefully separated.

Some say that we have no free will, but that it was destroyed by Adam; that we have some freedom of belief or faith, but none of doing or acting. But it was shown them that no man, not even Adam, had freedom from himself, but only as if from himself; and that everyone has freedom to act from the Lord, thus to be led by the Lord: and that each one is in this freedom so far as he is led. 219-1

All those preachers who in the life of the body have confirmed themselves in faith alone, and who cannot recede therefrom on account of their life, are not admitted to preach. Their priestly garment is taken away from them, and afterwards they do not know that they have been preachers. Very many are admitted to preach, but as soon as they preach faith separate from charity, and justification by it alone, all who are present go out, and the temple becomes empty. Thus those preachers who can recede from that faith are amended, and receive the doctrine of heaven. The case is similar with those who separate the Lord from the Father and do not make them one, and what is new, all of them, after they have been in the spiritual world a month, reject the third Person, acknowledging that the Holy Spirit is the Lord speaking through angels and spirits. The reason why they reject is because enthusiastic spirits, Quakers and many others, who are infernal, call themselves the holy spirit from eternity. I have had much speech with them in respect to this matter, to the effect that they have rejected the third Person of the Divinity, and that now they think of two, in order that they may see, whether from the two they make one.

One whom I knew in the world, had confirmed himself in faith alone by many arguments. I said to him that he should go and see those habitations in the desert, and when he went he saw nothing but a sandy waste, with rough stones and rocks all around, but not a single shrub nor a blade of grass; and, therefore, returning, he grieved over their miserable lot. There also he met and spoke with some who in the world had been acknowledged by him as learned men. And when he still wished to defend faith alone there appeared serpents which darted at his feet and coiled themselves around them. He was afterwards led to plains where those dwelt who were in a similar faith, where there was grass, shrubs, trees and buildings, and the inhabitants were of a cheerful disposition, and industrious in their work and business. They confessed that they had merely known of that faith from having heard it preached, but had thought nothing about it beyond the literal sense, and had not confirmed it any further; and that still they had lived a life according to the Word; thus that the faith was only a faith of science in their memory, but not a faith in the life. They are afterwards instructed and receive truths which they had not known in the world.

A learned man, who, in the world, had thought solely about faith alone, was examined as to whether he knew any truth of the church, whether he knew what faith is, or what the life of faith, what charity is, what love, what truth and the affection and perception of truth, what free will, what regeneration, what spiritual temptation, what Baptism, what the Holy Supper, what is heaven with man, and what and whence is hell, wherein is the holiness of the Word, what Providence is, what God and whether He is one or three, what conscience is, also what is the church in man and what heaven in him. And the angels heard; [and they saw] that he knew nothing of these things. The responses which he made were falsities derived from reasonings, and were also things from the Word which had been falsified. It was said to him, How could he be in the light of heaven, and hence in angelic wisdom, and from this in the felicity of heaven? Being convicted, he wished to learn, but because he had confirmed faith alone he could not.

I spoke with angels concerning the progression of truth to good, saying that the angels have joy when an infant or boy learns truths and acquires them from affection, thus when truths become truths of knowledge; they have greater joy when they become truths of the understanding, still greater when they become of the will, and the greatest joy when they become of the act. Then they love him because truths have taught him and led him to good. And they are gladdened when he knows that it is not truths which lead to good, but that it is good which leads him into truth and thus into wisdom. Man does not know this, but the angels perceive it and rejoice.

How Englishmen who wish to acquire a reputation for erudition compose their discourses with great elegance and as it were profound wisdom, especially concerning the influx of faith, and the endeavor to the doing of good, and of man's state then as to affection, reception and enlightenment by the Holy Spirit. Some of the English complained, saying that these elegancies delight their ears and are pleasing to them while they listen; but when they wish to apply anything therefrom to themselves they know not what the preachers have said, and whether it is allowable to adjoin the will, and thus to openly will, and act, or not. When they ask them, they say such sounding words as, that they may, and may not, and finally that it is a transcendent mystery. They speak in this manner so that their hearers, being able to gather either meaning from them, may praise them. And yet, by reason of these words with their double meaning in which something lies hidden like a snake in the grass, those hearers do not love them. They tell them that they should remain in the doctrine that is taught in the exhortation used at the Holy Supper, and that if they do not so from the will, the devil will, perchance, enter into them as he entered into Judas. Their discourses are also filled with the perception of trust and confidence in themselves.

I have sometimes heard it said from heaven that that faith saves no one because there is no life in it; and that true faith is truth; and that man has truth only so far as he shuns evils as sins. Particulars concerning the Decalogue and its Holiness, —See Spiritual Experiences.

The truths of faith are compared with the ornaments and utensils in palaces; unless man lives according to them they are, as it were, in a dark room with the windows shut, but as soon as a man lives according to them he is then elevated into heavenly light, the windows are opened, and he then sees those things and is delighted with them.

CONCLUSION. Lastly, it shall be told what the state of man is after death, whatsoever his religion may have been. They who have led a good life, who are such as have shunned evils because they are sins, and have conducted their business with rectitude and sincerity, are not let into the evils of their will, but are held by the Lord in good, and in intelligence and wisdom therefrom. But they who have lived in evil, are let into the evils of their will, and then they can think in no other way than in agreement with those evils; and when in that state, they appear as if insane, more like beasts than men. The love of doing evil then rules them, and they now rush into all things which they have coveted. They who have been in the love of ruling for the sake of self are more insane than others. I have seen many such spirits, and they appear as if utterly deprived of all rationality; and yet they then believe that they are wise, yea, the wisest of all. But it is allowed them at times to return into the rationality which they had in the world, when, from shrewdness, they had feigned themselves gifted with every virtue. Still, even then, the pleasure of returning into the delight of their will draws them on so that they cannot be led away except unwillingly; they wish to be insane. And because they are of such a character they are sent into hells, and then it is not permitted them to go out. And they there remain under the supervision of a judge who imposes tasks on them which they must do daily. If they do not perform them, they receive neither food, clothing, nor bed; and if they do evil they are severely punished. Thus by means of adequate tasks they are led away from the delights of their will. In such a prison all are held, both men and women, who have lived in evil, that is, who have given reins to their sins. But before they go, they are deprived of everything which they had formerly learned from the Word, and of everything which they had known concerning faith, and also of the knowledge of who they had been in the world, whether kings or magistrates, bishops or elders, rich or poor, or of the common people. And they are then all alike among themselves, nor is one greater than another. A low countryman may be together with an eminent man, nor does either know who had been the more eminent in the world; for elation of the mind exists equally with those who are of the common people as with those who are in the highest places. And, what is wonderful, they cannot go out to all eternity; for if, perchance, they put forth a foot, they are punished; and if they are taken out by others they become more insane than before. I have sometimes seen this done. They are like robbers who, from fear of punishment, live honestly in a house in a city, but as soon as they come into the woods they constantly think about robberies.

All the states of man can be recalled after death, the states of age, as the state of childhood, of adolescence and of youth; they who come into heaven come into the state of their adolescence, return into all the states of innocence, charity and affection with all their delights, and this with ineffable increase. With those who have lived well good states are recalled, with those who have lived in evil, evil states, concerning which various things have been said above.

That at this day they crucify the Lord, see Lord; and that they are like the Jews in their time: experience.

LOVE. From the ideas of spirits passing into the world of spirits after death, may be known all the ideas which they have had concerning God, heaven, love, and faith. Concerning God most of them have an idea as of a cloud or mist, because they have thought that God is a spirit, and of a spirit they have no other idea. Concerning heaven they have the idea that it is in the air, some that it is in the stars, others that it is in the universe, and scarcely any that it is with man; for they cannot remove the idea of space. Concerning heavenly joy they have ideas of delight, each one of the delight of his own love, especially of the delight of ruling and of living happily and continually in external luxuries. Few have an idea of living in internal delights; not knowing what they are. Concerning love they have so gross an idea that you may call it filthy. They think from the delight of the love of adultery. Some have no idea of love, because they have not known what love is. And so concerning mutual love; some have an idea of external friendship. In a word, all their ideas of love partake of the idea of lasciviousness. Concerning faith they have no other idea than as of the received faith, the quality of which has been spoken of above.

This is no idea of genuine faith since it is an idea of faith separated from charity, and what this is, is unknown. When the angelic idea concerning God, heaven, love, and faith flows in, if it is not perceived, it becomes in their minds like an obscure darkness; for the light of heaven does not enter in. Such, from faith alone, is the world at this day. For when that faith enters in and is received, then nothing of truth is loved. They say, "In this faith I know the truths of our church in one complex."

After death man comes into the world of spirits which is intermediate between heaven and hell; and there he changes his societies, and is thus prepared either for heaven or for hell. This change appears like a transference from one place to another, and also like a journey. He goes to various quarters, now ascending to higher regions, now descending to lower; and yet it is perceived that these journeys are only changes of state. This has been the case with me when I have been in the spirit. And at last when the man has been prepared, then that love leads him which is the head of his other loves. And he then turns his face to the society where his ruling love is, and thither he betakes himself as to his own home.

The knowledges of truth are inscribed on the affection or love, so that it is the affection that produces them as though they had been known to it. Affection sees those things which are consonant and concordant with itself, for some have the faculty of confirming. Wherefore if the affection is good, and it becomes good by means of life, it straightway has inscribed on it the knowledges which serve it; and when it hears and sees them, then, from things in itself which are similar and analogous, it discerns them; this therefore is of the love. But he who is in faith alone and in the love of self and the world, cannot be affected by other things than those which agree with his love; these are inscribed on his love. They are contrary to the truths of faith, which are: That God should be loved above oneself, heaven above the world, the good of the neighbor, and every use for the neighbor, and the like [above self]. The truths of faith are then cast out, which is also actually the case after death, and those things remain which are of the love, or, which are of the will.

All who are in the love of ruling for the sake of self and not for the sake of uses, retain that love after death; and wheresoever they come they wish to rule. This love rushes on as its bonds are relaxed. It spurns everything Divine, unless this afford it the means of ruling; in which case, so long as it serves as a means, it loves it; but when it does not serve as a means it not only rejects it but also holds it in hatred. The reason is, because this love is opposite to heavenly love. They are not admitted into heaven, and if, like hypocrites, they insinuate themselves into heaven they fill the whole neighborhood with an idea and image of themselves, and this even when they speak of God. This love turns aside the ideas of the angels, which are directed away from themselves and towards God; therefore they are driven away. This has been shown. For the most part they are corporeal because immersed in the proprium, and not elevated above it. Such spirits are taken to the boundaries of the world of spirits of our earth where there appears a lake smoking with fire; and first the spirit is rolled in the dust and let into his life in the world, and thus he is cast into the lake.

Let all who are in the world and read these lines know that the love of ruling for the sake of self and not for the sake of uses is diabolical love itself and in it are all evils. Let them know this and be on their guard. All evil loves are in that love and with it, even those of which the man had been wholly ignorant while in the world. I have examples in all abundance, showing that those who, in external form, appear to be moral and Christian men but interiorly in themselves have thought of nothing else but themselves and the world, after death are consociated with devils. There was one whom I saw during a long period of time, who was so haughty in his disposition that hardly anyone could be more haughty; and yet in the world he could talk with theologians and speak morally with other men; and he feigned justice and equity more than anyone else. But after death he became such a fiery devil that he not only denied God, but he also wished to be the devil himself, in order that he might continually fight against God and destroy heaven; and he was enflamed with hostility against all who were in the acknowledgment of the Lord. He was punished frequently, but in vain. If I should mention his deeds of malice, cunning, and crimes I would fill pages. In him I saw what the devil is, both in his own hell and with men (C. XII.). 234-1 Such men do not acknowledge God, but believe all are gods who are powerful; and they wish to become gods themselves, and be worshipped.

There was once some conversation respecting the love of ruling, to the effect that many believe that those who worship the Lord in the world, although they are His enemies, [will be saved and will rule over all in heaven]. 235-1 And it was said that a devil can be driven to worship the Lord, if only he be promised that he will be great, and still more if he would thereby become the greatest. It was then permitted that they should take from hell one of the devils there, who was most bitterly hostile to the Lord; and it was told him that he would be made the greatest by the Lord. He then put his whole mind to this object, and this to such a degree that he wished to lead all men to the Lord and to drive them by threats; saying, that the Lord alone should be honored and worshipped, and repeating it with earnestness and persuasion; but in his mind he cherished the thought that he would become the Lord's vicar. When, however, he saw that he had been deluded, he began to detest the Lord, and became as before, His most bitter enemy; but he was cast into hell. In a word, the delight of commanding exceeds every delight of the body.

Concerning the two rules or dominions, one from the love of self, the other from love towards the neighbor, see in the work on Heaven and Hell, in The Doctrine of the New Jerusalem, and in the little work on The Earths in the Universe, all of which works may be adduced.

With those who are in the love of commanding, the interiors appear black, and this because they are closed against the influx of heaven; but their inferiors appear as it were misty because they are opened to the hells. 237-1 It is said that with those who are in the love of ruling, the superiors, thus the interiors, can never be opened towards heaven.

There were seen men who belonged to the nobility of various nations. They had cordons lying over their breasts suspended from the shoulders, and also diadems. A number of them were seen. And being inspected by angels it was observed that they were continually directing their looks to themselves, and were thinking about their own superior eminence and excellence, and desiring that all men should turn their eyes to them. And because they believed that they were more worthy of being set over others than other men, therefore offices were given them. But when they were making conclusions with respect to subjects that concerned the common welfare, it was then perceived that they had no affection for the community, nor for uses; thus they were unable from judgment to discern good from evil, or truth thence from falsity, but could only speak in a high-sounding manner from the memory. And because they were of such a character they were cast out of their offices; and it was allowed them to wander about and get offices for themselves. But wherever they came they were told by the spirits there that they were thinking only of themselves and not of them, thus that they had no thought except what was from the sensual corporeal; therefore they were nowhere received. They did this for some time, afterwards I saw some of them reduced to extremities and seeking alms. Thus is the love of ruling brought low. One spirit who also wore the insignia of a nobleman confessed that as long as he wore that insignia he could not think as before, because he was interrupted by thought concerning himself; but whenever he was at home and put it off, he returned to his own judgment as before. 238-1 Diabolical spirits are skilled in the art of seducing the upright. They do this by turning their thoughts to themselves and their own proprium; by praising them in various ways; by placing themselves at their back and breathing into them the love of self; and where they observe anything black, which is the proprium, they inquire what is there; they then infuse it with their own thought and pervert, yea lead him. Some look into the forehead and act in like manner; others proceed in a different way. 238-2 Wherever blackness appears, there is the love of ruling, because this blackness is the proprium.

Love, which is of man's will, corresponds to flame, and faith, which is of the thought from the understanding, corresponds to light, this is derived from the Lord's influx from love and wisdom, or from the sun of heaven. From this sun proceed Divine love and Divine wisdom, love into the will and wisdom into the understanding. But only so much of intelligence [is received] as there is of love; just as is the case with light from flame.

They who worship the Lord from love, worship Him from all the truths of faith; therefore the more the truths the fuller and more acceptable is the worship. The reason is, because love excites all the things which have entered from love into the understanding. When the man is in worship only those things appear before him which he then speaks or prays, but all the rest are in vain and not in their series. When love produces truths, then these latter are disposed by the Lord into the form of heaven, and the man then adores the Lord as it were from heaven. This has been made known to me from experience in the spiritual world. When I see anyone, all those things come up which I know and have heard about him. The angels see these in their series, and so forth. Hence it is evident of what quality is the worship of the Lord by those who, from love to Him, are in genuine truths.

For the sake of instruction it sometimes happens that one spirit is allowed to change the affections in another, even into contrary affections; and according to the changes of his affections his face is changed so that it becomes wholly unrecognizable; there is also induced a monstrous form of face and also blackness according to the affections. Moreover, the body also is changed, becoming taller or shorter, taller from haughtiness and pride, and shorter from humility and the disparagement of self. It thence became evident that affection or love makes the man from head to foot. A like change takes place when a spirit is carried transversely through various societies, which was also seen, so that at length he is not recognized. Hence it is evident that he is altogether such as his love is. It was also shown that faith, which is of the thought, conjoined to corporeal love, and which also is various, makes man to be deformed according to the kind of love, and therefore in order that faith may be faith, it must be conjoined to spiritual affection.

The quality of the delight of the love of commanding was perceived, namely, that the sweetness within it is ineffable. From this sweetness man believes that it is heaven and heavenly joy, when yet it is hell. This delight is also turned into what is direful. It is similar with the love of doing evil, the love of hatred and revenge, the love of theft, and also the love of adultery, and their delights. Man does not know that when, by means of reformation by the Lord, these delights recede, then for the first time the delights of heaven enter in; which delights infinitely surpass the former. Nor does he know that the delights of those evils are then undelightful and stinging. Before reformation he does not know that such is their quality.

I saw many who had lived in this and former centuries, some of them military officers, of higher and lower rank, and others civil functionaries, all of whom, under the favoring influence of fortune, had contracted such a delight of commanding that they aspired to dominion over all things. Their delight was perceived as being to them like heaven. Moreover, they were gifted, above others, with talent and natural light in regard to civil affairs. After their decease, they had at first spoken about God; but after a short time they not only denied God and acknowledged nature; but at last they became like fools, sitting in dark shade; and in this way they led a miserable life. The reason is because the love of commanding is opposite to heavenly love.

After death every man is bound to many societies according to the number of his loves; but after vastation he comes into that society where his ruling love is, for this is the center of his other loves.

There was a certain man (Fr. G.) 245-1 who in his boyhood had cultivated piety, and who remained therefrom in the acknowledgment of God even to the end of his life. And yet under the favoring influence of fortune he came into the love of commanding and hence into evils of every kind. He did not indeed perpetrate them, but still he excused them and accounted them lawful. In the other life he prayed to God as he had done in the world, and with such fervor that scarcely anyone could pray more ardently; but it was to God the Father, for he believed that by doing this all things were forgiven him. But he began to burn with such hatred against the Lord that he denied Him; and afterwards he persecuted those who adored the Lord. At last he denied God and became like a fool; and he was sent among those who have little life.

They who are in the delight of the love of commanding cannot become spiritual. They become corporeal for the reason that they immerse everything of affection and hence of thought in their proprium, which in itself is corporeal and evil, so that they cannot be withdrawn from the proprium. Everyone who acknowledges God in heart, is elevated above his proprium; for man cannot look to God, acknowledging Him in heart, from himself; and he who cannot be elevated above his proprium has heaven closed to him. And since through heaven there flows in from the Lord intelligence, because it is spiritual light, therefore when heaven is closed they become stupid and like fools.

I once saw what kind of love to the Lord exists among Christians at this day. A number of them were let into their loves; and in phantasy it was granted them to see as it were the Lord. 247-1 And they then came into such fury that they wished to drag down and slay Him. They were all in faith alone, and, at the time, in the love of self. Thence it became evident that in the Christian world at this day they are against the Lord as were the Jews of old. In a word, all who are in faith alone and in the love of self and the world, and hence in evils, come into fury if they merely feel the Lord's Divine sphere.

THE JEWS. Before the Last Judgment, the Jews, for the most part, were at the left in the plane of the heel. I have often spoken with them there. They were then under the middle region where is the Christian world. 248-1 But after the Last Judgment they were driven away, and now being removed to the left, they dwell there in certain cities where the streets appear filled with filth and impurities, and where the houses are undergoing continual variation. This arises from the fact that newcomers are ever arriving and departing. They are there explored in order to find out who among them are able to acknowledge the Lord as the Messiah, whom they still look for in the world, and who are not. The former are taken to synagogues where they are instructed.

In that city an angel with a rod sometimes appears on high; and he gives them to believe that he is Moses. He exhorts them to desist from their madness in expecting the Messiah, when yet the Messiah is Christ, who, being now one with the Father, rules the whole heaven; adding that He knows this Himself, because He had known it in the world. They hear what he says; and when they depart those who cannot acknowledge, because of their life, forget it, but they retain it in their memory who can.

Of Abraham they have a Divine idea; of Jacob, and also of their fathers they have some Divine idea, but a lesser one. There is always set over them by the Lord, some converted Jew in whom Judaism lies hidden within or in the heart, and Christianity, without or in the mouth; and he is taught by certain angels from the Lord, in order that he may rule them according to their genius and disposition.

Footnotes
218-1 See SE 6023.
219-1 See SE 6024
234-1 See SE 4748, 4884.
235-1 The words in brackets are supplied from a corresponding passage in SE 4817.
237-1 See AC 1507.
238-1 See SE 5461 1/2.
238-2 See SE 5463.
245-1 See Se 5976, 5977.
247-1 See SE 4725.
248-1 See T 841.

They still retain from the world the carrying on of trade, especially in precious stones. These by certain methods they procure from heaven; for thence come precious stones, of which much more might be said. For in heaven are all things which are in the world. There is gold and silver there, also gold and silver in the form of coins, and also stones of every kind. Like all other things which appear before their eyes; they are from a spiritual origin, and hence are correspondences. They appear just as in the world. Divine truths are their origin; and therefore, with those angels who are in truths, the decorations in the houses are resplendent with silver and gold, and diamonds. Precious things of this kind are given from heaven to those below who are studious of truths; and because of their origin they also remain forever. The Jews get them from these and sell them. The reason why Jews have this business in the world, and also after their departure from the world, is because they love the Word of the Old Testament in the letter, and the literal sense of the Word corresponds to precious stones of various kinds. It is this sense that is meant by the twelve stones in Aaron's ephod, which were the Urim and Thummim; by the precious stones in Tyre, concerning which in Ezekiel; and by the precious stones with which the foundations of the wall of the New Jerusalem were adorned. Now because it was foreseen by the Lord that Christians would not hold the Old Testament so holy as do the Jews, therefore, the Jews have been preserved up to this day, and have been scattered throughout the whole Christian world, in order that the Word might still be in its holiness by means of correspondences. This also is the reason why it is still allowed the Jews to trade with similar things as in the world. If there had not been this reason, that whole nation, by reason of its perversity, would have perished.

There are also those who make precious stones for themselves artificially, so that they can scarcely be distinguished from the genuine. But these, when they are found out, are severely punished; they are put into a prison where they suffer harsh things, and are cast into the hells.

The Jews have no other delights than to acquire gain. Of interior delights they have no knowledge. Most of them are external men.

I have often spoken with the Jews on various subjects, namely, Concerning their sacrifices, that they refer to things heavenly; and in what way their various sacrifices signify the Lord. Concerning Isaac, why he might have been sacrificed by Abraham; and that these things had not been disclosed to them in the world because they were so external that they would not have received, for they were not willing to receive; and that they would have profaned them. Concerning the things which are contained in the fifty-third chapter of Isaiah. At this they became altogether silent; for the chapter was explained, so that they could make no answer. They were afraid lest it should be read again, for they were not willing to be convinced. Concerning eternal life, that it consists in the unanimity of all and in joy therefrom; and that as for them, they are at enmity with each other and thus cannot have the felicity of heaven. They answered, that they look for the Messiah who will unite them. I spoke with them about the signification of Jacob's sinew which was put out of joint, about Esau's heel which Jacob caught hold of, and about the heel which the serpent bruised, that these signify themselves; about their origin from a Canaanitish woman, and from whoredom with a daughter-in-law. And it was explained what all these signify, and that the things there meant are such as are signified. Then that the Jews and their tribes mentioned in the Word are not they but are things celestial and spiritual. I spoke about the land of Canaan, to the effect that they believe they are to be introduced into that land by the Messiah when He comes; that He will walk before them with a rod, and will dry up the rivers; that a wall of fire will be round about them; that they will go through Christendom, and that Christians will take hold of their garments and beg to be allowed to follow them; and that they will admit these and hold them as slaves provided they give their money; and many similar things. They were asked whether the dead and those in the world of spirits are also to follow the Messiah, or whether it is only those who are in the world; whether the land of Canaan would be able to hold them; where the Messiah was to be born; whether they knew the line of David, or the situation of Bethlehem; and many similar questions; why they look for an earthly kingdom when the kingdom of the Messiah is a heavenly one, which those who have now departed from the world might know. All this was said and heard. Those of them who were evil could not be convinced, but some who were upright wished to be instructed. It was explained to them what the land of Canaan signifies, and what Jerusalem; why these are called holy; what Zion signifies; what the twelve tribes represent and hence signify; also the passages where it is said that they who had been in captivity would return, to the effect that it was by no means they who were meant, but that it was so written on account of the spiritual sense in each particular. I spoke with them about the spiritual sense; at which they first said that they knew there was a mystical sense in the Word, and that they knew that mystical sense, which was that they receive gold and that they are able to make gold. To which I answered that, mystically, that is, spiritually, this is also true, because gold signifies the good of love, and they who are in that mystical or spiritual sense of the Word, receive this love. But they wanted gold, not love, saying that the possession of gold is love. 254-1

Before the Last Judgment they called the two cities Jerusalem. But after the Judgment they changed the name by command; because the name Holy Jerusalem, mentioned in Revelation, then came everywhere into general use; by which is signified the New Church into which none shall enter who does not make the Messiah one with Jehovah, thus only he who worships the Lord alone. The Jews are treated of in the Arcana Coelestia.

The Jews strive much after heaven, believing that heaven is theirs, and that to inherit the land is to inherit heaven, that the land of Canaan is in heaven, and that the Messiah is with them. They marvel that He does not descend to them from heaven, but I answered that He does not will to do this because there is so much discord among them and such enmities and hatreds, and contempt for others; and because they pray to the God of Israel not for the sake of salvation but that they may become rich.

Those of them who are evil are cast down into the hells which are under their great tract; many into woods and deserts where they commit robbery, but still they are miserably punished. The Word is taken away from them.

They have been preserved also for the sake of the Hebrew language. They also have the Word written in the ancient Hebrew language where all the letters are curved, because in such a letter the Word has a more immediate communication with heaven.

THE TEN COMMANDMENTS. Ten articles, what is effected with man when he fights against evils as sins, as before.

Then the commandments of the Decalogue, where the evils are which are sins, against which one must fight. —Then of the spiritual which is then given to him, and in which he also comes; there is the spiritual there in every precept.

What charity is, is; it is to do uses, everyone in his own function.

What faith out of charity is, and what faith from charity is.

Something concerning faith separated from charity, what its quality is when man is in it both as to life and doctrine.

OBSERVATIONS CONCERNING FAITH. In a particular small work faith will be treated of, thus concerning faith separated from charity, after the work on the Last Judgment, in which all things will be described by articles, which are:

What charity and faith are.

One cannot be separated from the other. There is no charity where there is no faith, and there is no faith where there is no charity.

As far as there is one, so far there is the other, in equal degree and in equal quality.

Faith is truth.

Faith does not produce charity, but charity faith. —Before there is charity, those things which are supposed to be of faith, are only knowledges without life.

Faith without charity is not possible. —Faith without charity is no religion. —Faith without charity falsifies the Word. —Faith without charity blinds all the understanding of truth. —It is the end of the church when there is not the faith of charity. —Every church ends in Babylon, and in faith separate. —Faith separate from charity is predicted in the Apocalypse, and is meant by the dragon and his two beasts. —Faith without charity is meant by the he-goat in Daniel and in Matthew. —Faith without charity is meant by Philistea. —Faith without charity is meant by Cain. —Faith without charity is meant by Reuben. —Faith from charity, also faith without charity, is meant by Peter. —Charity is meant by James, and the works of charity by John.

The quality of the faith of the present day is to be presented, such as it is, and the degrees of justification such as they are, they are to be described briefly, and that it is the whole of theology at the present day, also that if it is confirmed there arise many falsities, but not if it is not confirmed.

The will is double, spiritual and natural. Knowledges are the storehouse of faith. All things of faith can be seen. Falsities of faith are not faith. Faith is truth.

. THE LAST JUDGMENT. What the Last Judgment is.

The Last Judgment has been effected three times.

The Last Judgment was effected and is effected by the Lord from firsts by ultimates.

The Last Judgment could not have been effected the second time, unless He Himself had come into the world, and by that as (in firsts) be also in ultimates.

Without the Last Judgment effected by Him, thus without His Coming into the world, no one of mortals could have been saved.

Unless the Lord had glorified His Human, even to its ultimates, no Last

Judgment could be effected at this day. —Thus hereafter no one could be saved.

After the Last Judgment a new church is always to be established and is established, and before [the Last Judgment] it could not be nor can it be.

Therefore it is predicted in the Apocalypse, that the New Jerusalem will descend from heaven after the Last Judgment, by which is meant the New Church.

No one is received in that church thus in heaven, after this except he who acknowledges God, one in Person and Essence, in whom is the Trinity, thus the Lord; and unless by some combats he has removed and shunned evils as sins against the Divine laws.

THE ENGLISH. The English have a double theology, one for the learned and one for the unlearned.

The preachers compose their discourses so that the learned understand their theology and the unlearned theirs, and this is done from a certain fear on account of reputation and favor on both sides.

To the question whether they believe that the theology for the unlearned is true, they reply that they do not know otherwise when they utter that prayer in their temples, but not so when they compose their discourses.

It is then said to them, that the reason they do not know otherwise at that time is from influx out of heaven; and that it is not so when they compose their discourses, is from influx from their proprium; because they then think concerning themselves, their own learning, and fame and favor there from.

VARIOUS THINGS CONCERNING THE SPIRITUAL WORLD. Various things concerning those things which are in the Spiritual World, from which some things have been quoted in the Continuation Concerning the Spiritual World. To Be Observed. LEIBNITZ AND WOLFF. I spoke with John Wolff and his preceptor Leibnitz concerning the simple substance and preestablished harmony.

Concerning the simple substance Leibnitz said, that his opinion concerning the monad was never like that of Wolff concerning the simple substance. He said that he indeed acknowledged monads as unities but that there were in them simpler and purer substances by which the monad was formed, from which changes of state existed therein; since if there were nothing therein, it would be nothing, in which there cannot be any change of state, for a vacuum admits of no change. Leibnitz therefore wondered that Wolff held that his monad, which he calls a simple substance, was created out of nothing, and that when divided it falls into nothing; and yet he had attributed changes of state to it; and also that he had called some existences simple substances, and which are in nature, which anyone can see are aggregations of substances, like the parts of the air and ether, the elements of metals, and also souls. Wolff said that he wished by his definitions of his simple substances to captivate the minds of theologians, who want it to be believed that all things have been created by God out of nothing, immediately; at that time not knowing that his followers, by confirming these principles in themselves, would close in themselves the ways to angelic wisdom, which nevertheless are founded on natural truths.

Concerning preestablished harmony, Leibnitz said, he had considered and deduced it from this, that thought acts as one with man's speech, countenance, and action; and at that time he had not thought of interior thought, from which many men do not speak nor act; and which with many combats with the exterior; and still less did he think of spiritual thought, into which man does not come until after death; then that he considered nothing else in the world but thought, which at that time he acknowledged in place of the soul; and he did not consider affection at the same time, from which and according to which he thinks. Therefore now, after he has been instructed by angels he confesses that he erred, and he knows that the case is altogether otherwise.

NEWTON. I spoke with Newton concerning a vacuum, and concerning colors.

Concerning a vacuum he said, that in the world he had believed in the existence of a vacuum; but when the angels perceived that he had an idea of a vacuum, as an idea of nothing, they turned themselves away, saying that they cannot bear the idea of nothing, since when there is an idea of nothing the idea of the essence of things perishes. And when the idea of the essence of things perishes, the idea of thought, understanding, affection, love, and of will with men and angels perishes, which things are not given in nothing. They asked him whether he believed that the Divine, whence is all angelic wisdom, and all intelligence to men in both worlds, the spiritual and the natural, is a vacuum, and thus that any Divine operation inflows through a vacuum into their vacuum and can present itself to perception. At that question he was disturbed. He replied that it cannot through an absolute vacuum, which is nothing, but through an apparent vacuum, because the Divine is the Esse itself of wisdom and love with the angels in heaven and with men in the world, and it fills all things. Also Esse itself and nothing are so contrary to each other, that if one be admitted the other cannot. Therefore the angels entreated that he and all those who cherished the idea of a vacuum as of nothing would desist from it, that they might be together, knowing that nothing of their life can ever be given in nothing, but in those things which are, and which are or exist from the Esse. They added that not anything can be said of a vacuum which is nothing, which has relation to acting, reacting, receiving, or attracting, thus to the life of their wisdom and love; in which there are so many infinite affections with their variations, perceptions, and sensations; for nothing is nothing, and of nothing we cannot predicate something. When he had heard these things, Newton said that before this he had desisted from that idea, and he would desist from it hereafter; knowing that he is now in the spiritual world, in which, nevertheless, according to his former idea, would have been his vacuum; and that even now he is a man, and therein he thinks, feels, acts, yea breathes, and this could not take place in a vacuum which is nothing, but in something which is, and from Esse exists and subsists, and that an interstitial nothing is impossible, because that would be destructive of something, that is of essences and substances which are something. For something and nothing are altogether opposites, even so that he was horrified at the idea of nothing, and would beware of it, lest his mind fall into a swoon.

Concerning colors he said that in the world he had believed that they originated from the substances, as it were, of different colored materials continually flowing forth from the solar ocean, and adding themselves continually to like things in objects in the world, likewise when they pass through pellucid objects following then the ways of light, according to its diffractions and refractions, and proceeding as like to like, thus red to red, blue to blue, yellow to yellow, and so on, as in prisms, crystalline globes, and vapors whence come rainbows. But the angels did not acknowledge this cause of colors, saying that there are colors in the spiritual world as well as in the natural world; and in the spiritual world they are vivid, splendid, and variegated more than in the natural world, and that they know that they are variegations of their light corresponding to their love or good, and to their wisdom or truth, and that the sun from which their light proceeds, is the Lord Himself, whose Divine love presents around Him the appearance of a sun, and the Divine wisdom therefrom the appearance of light, and that from that sun, which as was said, is pure love, no such substances or matters flow forth, but that pure light presents to view variegations of colors in objects according to the reception of wisdom by the angels; the color red according as their wisdom is derived from good, and the color bright white according as their wisdom is derived from truth, and the rest as they partake of the defect and absence of them, which there correspond to shade in the world. Moreover the angels, by their spiritual ideas, by which they are able to present and bring forth the causes of things to the life and to full consent, demonstrated that colors are nothing else than variegations of flamy light and bright white light, in objects according to their forms; and that colors are not materials, so neither is light, because they correspond to the love and wisdom of the angels, from whom they proceed by Divine operation; and their love and wisdom are not material but spiritual. Neither are heat and light in the world material, but natural, and they inflow into matters, and they modify themselves in them according to the forms of the parts. Therefore neither are colors material, as they would be if they existed from different colored atoms. At length from some indignation they said, "Who cannot see a paradox in the Newtonian cause, yea what is absurd?" And they departed, saying they would return if he would discern spiritually or even naturally concerning colors, and not so materially and sensually. Then some spirits approached, and said to him, "We entreat you to think of colors not as originating from some small prism or from some wall, but from the green color of all the woods and grassy fields of the whole world in which you were; can you conceive of a continuous efflux from the sun of a green color alone, and at the same time an influx, and a continual restoration, likewise of a continual influx of gray or stone color into the mountains of the whole earth, and so on? Can you then conceive of a continuous ocean of green alone, and of rock color alone? Tell us where they go, where they subsist, do they proceed into the universe? Or do they fall downwards somewhere, or ascend upwards? From these things perchance new earths exist, for they must be in great abundance because they are material." After he thought of this thing more deeply, he said, "Now I know that colors are modifications of light in objects, in the forms of which they make general planes, upon which the light is variegated according to the forms of the parts, whence are colors." These are the words of Newton himself, which he wishes me to communicate.

LONDON. London in the spiritual world appears like the London in the natural world as to its streets and quarters, but is dissimilar as to houses and habitations; this difference is not apparent, because everyone there dwells in a quarter and in a house corresponding with his affection and thought thence derived. In the middle of the city is situated the Royal Exchange. To the right of it dwells the moderator, and round about it his officers. The middle street of it answers to Holborn; the east is in front, toward the back even to Wapping is the west; the south is at the right of that street; and the north is on its left. In the eastern quarter, which is of considerable length, reaching far beyond the city, dwell the best of them, where they all worship the Lord. Those who are distinguished for intelligence dwell in the southern quarter which extends almost to Islington, where there is also an assembly. They who dwell there are also prudent in speaking and writing. Towards the north those dwell who are illiterate, and who are in the greatest degree of liberty of speech which they love. In the west are those who are in the obscure affection of good. Those who are there are fearful of manifesting their thoughts. In the southern region answering to Moorfield's and round about it, is a promiscuous multitude; thither from the city are sent away all those who incline to evils, wherefore the multitude there is cast out by turns, and thus continually, through this way the city is continually purified, and those who are led away therefrom appear no more. Sometimes they see about the middle of the city a certain malicious person sitting on a seat in a pulpit, and the inhabitants are called together and ordered to go thither to him. They who approach and hearken are led to the place of exit, where there are promiscuous crowds, and as was said, they are sent out through the ways there. Every society is purified, this is the manner of purifying them there. Their houses, clothing, and food are similar to those used in the world. I asked about wine, strong drink, beer, chocolate, tea and the like, and was told that they had similar things. I asked also about the liquor called punch, they said that they also have that liquor, but it is given only to those who are sincere and at the same time industrious. They do not tolerate in the city any ruler who directs or dictates to them what they must do, for they wish to be in full liberty.

The English live together, and do not travel about in other regions, for they are of a different genius and disposition from others, and their disposition is such, that they do not admit others into intimacy with them.

It was also shown to them that they speak, write and think spiritually, and that they themselves do not know otherwise than that they do all things naturally; from which they were instructed by me that there is no ratio between the spiritual and the natural, thus there is no conjunction through what is continuous, but through what is discrete, that is, by correspondences; which conjunction makes a likeness as if they are one. They were a little envious that they had not discovered this. Moreover in each degree there is an internal and an external, and the external corresponds to the internal, and the externals are appearances like material things, although they are not material. It was shown to them also by ascent to the third heaven, that there is a similar difference between the celestial and the spiritual, as there is between the spiritual and the natural so that there is no ratio between them, that is, the natural cannot become spiritual by any continuous purification, nor can the spiritual become celestial, thus not by any approximation, but it is like the difference between cause and effect or between the soul and the body.

I afterwards spoke with them concerning priests. And I saw that there is one kind of priests that supposes they are more erudite and learned than others. These all dwell in the west, and when they come to preach, they go forth from the west a little into the north, and so towards the middle of the city to the temples. This is a sign that they go in the way of taciturnity and ignorance, for in the west those dwell who are taciturn, and there near to the north those who are ignorant of truth. They appear to themselves to preach learnedly and with erudition, because they preach about the Divine operation into the actions of men, when they are justified; thus concerning the effort, which is the fourth degree of justification, which inflows into the act with men, they themselves being ignorant of it, and that the voluntary of man is not present, since that is evil. The hearers complained of them that they cannot understand them whether they wish them to act of themselves or not; because they can take both senses from their ambiguous teachings. It was perceived that they wish such discourses to sound learned before preachers and bishops, and that they do not dare to preach otherwise before them. But there are also preachers who dwell in the south, who altogether preach that they must shun evils as from themselves, and that they must do goods as from themselves; but that still they must know that they are not from themselves, thus the citizens love these; they speak in harmony with the prayer before the Holy Supper.

In the suburbs at the left dwell many of their learned and with them Newton, they go down thither by a sloping way.

In a word they who teach according to their prayer at the Holy Supper, dwell in the south towards the east, and they are loved because they think as they preach, the rest do not, but dispute continually with them, and reply that they cannot do otherwise. I saw them recede to their habitations in the west, which are at the right side there where there is a place of exit, and some also are led out.

It was said of those preachers in the west, that they do not care to know evils or sins, because God knows, and not they, nor do they wish to know from affection any other knowledges than what confirm their faith. They despise those who are in the south and east as simple, who as it were with their thought are low; and that their thought is not elevated but depressed, when yet it is altogether contrary.

I heard a conversation with presbyters in the west, which was effected by representatives. On one side the devil with hell was represented, on the other side the Lord with heaven, and then it was said, that the devil or hell dwells in the evils with man, and that the Lord with heaven is in the goods with him. Then that the Lord through heaven continually drives away the devil with hell. But the man who excuses his evils, and who lives in them, retains with himself the devil with hell, nor does he permit him to go away, although the Lord drives him away. Also the devil then speaking with him, says what need is there to know evils, so as to combat against them, when God does that? and so he confirms man, therefore he is retained and thus they live together as friends; besides many similar things. Also the devil by that faith confirms them, saying what need is there of other knowledges, than those which belong to that faith? they are of no help; what need is there to know evils, because man from himself cannot combat against them? What need is there of combats, because man of himself can do nothing? When nevertheless everything of life, everything of reason, and everything of freedom man has from the Lord, and He wills that man should act as of himself, and without man's cooperation as of himself, the evil remains, and the devil with evil, etc.

Those priests in the west complained that those who were in faith alone, or in faith separated, disappeared, saying that they do not know where they went, some said that they saw some in the hells.

Footnotes
254-1 See T 845; SE 2256, 2257, 4388.

THE MORAVIANS. I do not write of those who are in the world, but of those who are out of the world, I spoke with these and I heard. They are mere Arians, and deny the Divine of the Lord, saying that He has the Divine, such as man has. When it was said to them that He was conceived of Jehovah, they come together, nor do they wish easily to admit it, wishing to deny the Scripture lest they should be refuted; but still they say something that the Jews do. Others when they are convinced, say that He was born that He might be adopted. They confirm themselves by the Lord's word that in His freedom He was left to suffer the cross, not knowing why this was done. They say that they love Him, because He took it upon Himself to suffer the cross, and also because it is commanded by the Father, then especially because He is loved by the Father on account of the passion of the cross. They reject the Old Testament as no longer for them but for the Jews. They also despise the Gospels, saying that the Lord is spoken of as a simple man, and thus that there is nothing Divine in them. Concerning faith in Him spoken of in the Gospels, they say that He so wished it, and that it ought not speak thus. They acknowledge the Epistles of Paul only, and also the historicals of the Word, but they do not believe in the holiness of the Word. They say concerning good works and charity, that they ought not to be together with faith, and that they shudder at doing good works for the sake of heaven, and that in their heaven they would rather adopt the most malevolent than such; in a word they condemn them to hell. In speaking they utter the greatest fallacies; they speak with each one according to his heart in religion. They guard lest those mysteries should be disclosed; the rest which are concerning the Holy Supper and Baptism they think and teach violently. They are such things as do not agree with the faith of the Reformed, nor do they admit to the Holy Supper any others than those who receive those three mysteries, because they have confirmed them. From these things it is evident that they are among the worst who profess Christianity. They make much of their sensation, but it was shown to them, that their sensation is with their spirits, who were enthusiastic spirits from their assembly in the world, who come nearer to them, who think much of their religion and love it, saying that they are more loving and happy than others. These confirm them very greatly, thence is their sensation.

They are held in the lower earth to the left in a society separated from the rest; because they are among themselves, and they are a society of interior friendship, which if it should be in the neighborhood of others, they would destroy their delights. They recede by turns from that society towards the left, into a desert which is for them alone, where there is no grass, where there are crags and cliffs.

THE DUTCH. How formally and courteously they invite their wives and bring and lead them to their house, and show how well it is with those who act together in unity in their houses, and also how clean and well furnished their houses are; and on the contrary how unclean those are where there is the dominion of one over the other; savory food is also given those who act in unity, and they are taught by these things the quality of their delight when one is of the other mutually and reciprocally. Therefore when they see those things and apperceive them to be true they desist from dominion; and then they obtain a habitation nearer to the middle, and are led into a house better furnished. The reason is that there is then conjugial love, which regarded in itself is celestial love itself.

THE MORAVIANS IN LONDON, THE HERRENHUTERS AND THE JEWS. The Moravians dwell in the furthest corner of the place of exit mostly at the side there, but when they journey into the city as to their sanctuary, they appear to proceed towards the middle and thence a little to the south, and thus to their corner, which is done because they wish to appear to others as Christians, of a similar doctrine. Afterwards from their corner they go into the west where the presbyters are who are in faith alone, concerning whom we have before spoken, and they return thence. From their corner, which is as it were their inn there, they go out by turns, and descend into a vault which stretches deeply under the west, where the presbyters are of whom we have before spoken, and their hell is there, from which they are no longer let out, except some into deserts. It is not allowed them to dwell near others, nor elsewhere, because they form a society of interior friendship, which takes away the spiritual delight of others. They say to others that they should dwell here and there even to the middle, but still they dwell at that corner, of which they have an idea as of their inn. They appear in a way towards the middle, because they persuade that they are of the Anglican religion and speak with the English piously as if they were; and that they differ only as to ceremonials, which are like those of the Apostles. When they are asked why their preachers are clothed in blue, they say because that color is loved; nor do they dare to say that they should be clothed like the English preachers in a black gown, because they fear lest their mysteries should be disclosed. They very greatly fear to be sincere and just on account of religion. They are altogether averse to this, wherefore they are prone to all kinds of evils, taking care only lest they be discovered, because with others this would be hurtful to their religion.

Moreover the Jews do not dwell upon the earth in London, but under the earth there, on the northern side below, where Towerhill is. They enter there through a dark opening. And the citizens of the city do not know where they dwell.

THE LOVE OF KNOWING. The love of knowing is the external of the will, the use on account of which [it is done] is the internal of the will.

With infants and boys the external rules, in process of time the internal is formed. [Marginal Note:] Use of life makes the internal of the will originating from the sun of heaven. It [that is the exterior] is as in the time of winter, and like what is foul shining exteriorly.

Then there is formed the love of knowing for the sake of use, these are formed whether they are good or evil.

But the love of understanding whether a thing is true or not, and thence the love of being wise, is also the external of the will, originating from the light of heaven and its variegation.

This love, because it is the external of the will, can be separated from its internal, and then it is the love of one's own glory, on account of glory and not on account of any use then. Therefore it can be given also with the evil.

Or the external of the will in the understanding is the love of truth on account of glory, thus on account of the external.

THE JEWS. The Jews less than others know that they are in the spiritual world. They think there of the Messiah as they did in the world and expect Him. And they say that He will come. But when it is said to them that it will be in Bethlehem, and from the house of David, and they are asked where is Bethlehem now, and where is the house of David, they do not know how to answer other than that He knows where that city is, and where that family is. Some of them in the other life say that the Messiah is in heaven, and that He will not come to those in the spiritual world before He is born a boy in the world. When they are asked whether they only who are in the world will be led into Canaan, they reply that they will then return into the world, and they will dwell with them in the land of Canaan. When they are asked whether they will then be again born, they say they will not, but that they will descend to them, believing that thus they will be men like them. When they are asked whether Canaan will be capacious enough for all who have been born from that nation from the time of Abraham, they say that the land of Canaan will then be enlarged. When they are asked how the Messiah, the Son of Jehovah, can dwell with such evil persons, they say that they are not evil. When it is said that Moses in his song said that they were the worst, and do they read it and sing it as was commanded by Moses, they reply that Moses was angry when he wrote that, because they departed from him, and therefore they do not read it, but run through it quickly. When it is said to them that their origin is from a Canaanitess, and from whoredom with a daughter-in-law, they then are angry and depart, saying that it is enough that they are from Abraham and Jacob. They say that Moses and David will also return and go with the Messiah, one at His right and the other at His left. They narrate many fabulous things concerning the Messiah, how He will introduce them into the land of Canaan, and how rich Christians will follow them freely, if they give them their money. Nevertheless many of them who know that Christ who is the Messiah rules all things in the heavens, say that they wish to receive this, but cannot; they hear it from Moses, who sometimes appears above with a rod, and teaches this, and when they hear, they go away in various directions. They said to me, "Why did He suffer the cross?" I replied, "Because He was the greatest prophet, and therefore He carried the iniquities of the people, like the prophet who lay on his right side and on the left, and ate bread made of barley and filth, of whom it is said that he bore their iniquities; likewise other prophets, one who took a harlot to wife, who put on ashes, who went barefoot, who thus bore their iniquities; in like manner it is said of the Messiah" (Isa. 53). When they heard this they said that they would go off among themselves and consult together. They who have not become foul from filthy avarice, and who have not become devils from hatred, fraud and revenge, are tolerated below the heavens where their habitations are, because they regard the Word as holy, and they who suffer themselves to be instructed concerning the Lord, are transferred to societies where they are instructed, and are sent back to those who have not yet received. Their business is dealing in diamonds and precious stones as in the world. They procure them for themselves from heaven. They learn that they have that business, because they regard the Word as holy, because the sense of the letter corresponds to those stones and signifies them. Therefore the more holy they regard the Word, the better do they succeed there in that business.

DEGREES. There is a natural kingdom, a spiritual kingdom, and a celestial kingdom.

In the natural kingdom are men whilst they live in the world. In the spiritual kingdom are spiritual angels; in the celestial kingdom are celestial angels; for there are these three universals, the natural, the spiritual, and the celestial.

In each kingdom there are two degrees, in the natural two, in the spiritual two, and in the celestial two; thus in the three kingdoms there are six degrees. All these degrees are discrete, or discontinuous, and are called degrees of altitude. Discrete degrees are to each other as thought to speech, or as the affection to gesture, or as the affection of the mind to the countenance; and in the material world as the ether to the air, or as a nerve to the fibers of which it is composed. All compositions in the whole natural world and in the spiritual world are of this character, and they consist either of two or three degrees of this kind in their order. These degrees are called prior and posterior, higher and lower, interior and exterior; and, in general, they are as cause and effect, or as a substance and a substantiate, or as the aggregate from substances, or as a principle and the principiates, or the thing formed from principles.

There are also continuous or cohering degrees; each discrete degree has its continuous degree. The continuous degree of each discrete degree is as light verging to shade, and at length to the obscurity of night; and also as the rational thought which is in light to sensual and, as it were, at length to corporeal thought, which is in a dense shade according as it descends to the body. In such a degree continually decreasing is the human mind. In a similar degree, but lower; are man's sight, hearing, smell, taste, and touch; in like manner his speech and his singing; for man has a tone like the tone of a lyre, and like the sound of a drum. It is also similar with harmonies and beauties; for they proceed by continuous degrees from the highest harmony and beauty, to the least. These degrees are of the cause in itself and of the effect in itself; they are distinguished from the former degrees, because these are of the cause and the effect in themselves. Continuous degrees are called degrees of what is purer or grosser. An idea of these degrees can be had chiefly from light and shade, and also from the aerial atmosphere in its lower and higher regions; for in the lower region it is grosser, denser, and more compressed, and in the higher region it is purer, rarer, and more extended.

Unless one procures a knowledge of these two kinds of degrees, he cannot have an idea of the interiors and exteriors of man, thus neither of the soul and the body, nor indeed of causes and effects. Nor can he have an idea of the distinction between the heavens, nor of the wisdom of the angels in the heavens; nor can he have any idea of correspondences, of representatives, of influx, of order, thus he cannot have an idea of those things which are of order, both in the natural world and in the spiritual world, thus scarcely any just idea of anything.

Few hitherto have had any other idea of degrees than of continuous degrees, which is, as was said, from what is pure to what is gross, or from greatest to least. From which it follows that only one kind of degrees has been known, and that the natural degree and the spiritual degree are distinguished only as what is pure and gross; in like manner the difference between the heavens, and also in the wisdom of the angels. Whereas the difference is according to discrete degrees, the nature of which we shall presently show from experience.

There are, therefore, as stated above, six discrete degrees, two in the natural kingdom, two in the spiritual kingdom, and two in the celestial kingdom; but these degrees are those in which men and angels are, as to their thoughts, their affections, and their wisdom therefrom. Degrees are as follows: Below these six degrees of life, there follow similar degrees, and also material, even to the ultimate, and above those six degrees ascend degrees of the infinite even to the Divine itself. For the Divine itself cannot flow into any angel or man from itself but by discrete degrees; for if it flowed in immediately, or by what is continuous, both angel and man, from the ardor of the Divine love, and from the light of the Divine wisdom, would be entirely consumed. This would be as though the sun, of the world, from its fire, were to flow immediately into the objects of the earth, and not mediately through the atmospheres according to distinct discrete degrees.

There are three natural atmospheres arising from the sun of the world, and there are three spiritual atmospheres arising from the sun of heaven, which is the Lord. The three natural atmospheres arising from the sun of the world are the purer ether, which is universal, from which is all gravitation; the middle ether, which forms the vortex around the planets, in which are the moons and the satellites, from which is magnetism; and the ultimate ether which is the air. By these three atmospheres all the corporeal and material things of the earth are held together, which are so composed as to be applicable to those three degrees. The three spiritual atmospheres arising from the sun of heaven, are those in which are the angels of the three heavens. In the two higher atmospheres are the angels of the Lord's celestial kingdom; in the third and the first natural, which is pure ether, are the angels of the Lord's spiritual kingdom, and in the atmospheres following those two which are the middle and the ultimate ether, which is the air, are men while they are in the natural world.

But it should be known, that the atmospheres arising from the sun of heaven, which is the Lord, properly speaking, are not three, but six, there are three above the sun of the world, and there are three below it. The three below the sun of the world constantly accompany the three natural atmospheres, and enable a man in the natural world to think and to feel. For the atmospheres arising from the sun of the world have not life in themselves, because they originate from a sun which is pure fire; but the atmospheres arising from the sun of heaven, which is the Lord, have life in themselves, because they originate in the sun, which is pure love and pure wisdom. The atmospheres which originate from the sun of the world, which is pure fire, cause those things on the earth, and in the human body, to subsist and be held in connection together, and they are not changed except according to the laws of natural order. Hence is the difference between things in the natural world and in the spiritual world, concerning which difference more will be said in what follows.

That in the spiritual world which is above the natural world, there are also atmospheres, is evident from the light and heat there, which before the eyes and senses of the angels appear similar to the light and heat before the eyes and senses of men; and angels are spiritual, but men are natural, and there cannot possibly be any light and heat with their differences without atmospheres. That there are also spiritual atmospheres is evident from many appearances in the spiritual world, as from the appearance of colors there, of meteors, of clouds both thin and thick, of winds, of gravities, pressures, and consequent consistencies, which although they appear entirely similar to such things as are in the natural world, nevertheless, they are spiritual and not natural; although before the angels, because they are spiritual, they appear similar. That there are spiritual atmospheres, is evident especially from the respiration of angels and spirits. For angels and spirits breathe in like manner as men in the world; but angels breathe from their atmospheres, and men from theirs. The angels in the celestial kingdom breathe from their atmosphere which is more pure, but the angels of the spiritual kingdom breathe from their atmosphere which is less pure.

But the things which we have hitherto said concerning degrees and atmospheres are, for the most part, theoretical; but all theoretical things should be drawn and concluded from the facts of experience, and also be confirmed by them. For unless the facts of experience, as it were, lead the hand of man in coming to conclusions, he may be deceived in theoretical things, and from some imaginary hypothesis, be carried away into false principles entirely opposed to what is true, which he can then confirm by fallacies and appearances of every kind; for false principles may be confirmed by appearances and fallacies to such a degree, that a man may believe that they are truths themselves. I wish, therefore, now to produce some facts of experience, by which not only what has been said may be confirmed, but also by which everyone who is in the light of the mind or who has natural ability, may draw conclusions as to many other things.

In the natural kingdom in which men are whilst they live in the world, and in the spiritual kingdom where the spiritual angels are, and in the celestial kingdom in which are the celestial angels, similar things appear, so much so that there is scarcely any other difference than that the like things in the spiritual kingdom are more perfect than in the natural kingdom, and in the celestial kingdom still more perfect than in the spiritual kingdom. A spirit or an angel appears like a man in the world, even so that he knows no otherwise than that he is a man of the world. He has a similar face and a similar body, and in the face similar eyes, nostrils, ears, lips, mouth, and similar hair; and in the body also a similar breast, abdomen, loins, hands and feet, and also similar organs of generation; in a word, he is a man in external form altogether like a man of the world. He has similar lungs, because he breathes; and he has a similar heart, because it pulsates. The other interior viscera of the body are also similar, because there are societies in heaven which equally correspond to these viscera. There is likewise a ruddiness in the face, hands, arms, and body, as if from blood in the arteries and veins. There are also similar fibers, nerves, and muscles, because in like manner a spirit moves his limbs like a man in the world. Moreover, he has similar sight, hearing, smell, taste and touch. He also has similar speech and singing; he has also a similar power of imagination, thought, intellect, and will, also affection and cupidity. In a word, an angel or a spirit is so similar to a man of the world, that he himself knows no otherwise than that he is a man of the world. Conjugial love is also similar with all its effect; moreover there is not propagation, but in place of it union of minds, and thence an increase of intelligence and wisdom. Thence it is that in the Word in its spiritual sense by marriage is meant the conjunction of truth and good, and by daughters goods, and by sons truths, and so on.

Their garments also are similar to the garments of men; they have tunics, mantles, breeches, stockings, shoes, caps, tiaras and undergarments like those in the world, with some difference as to colors, especially of the tunics. The reason is, because colors signify the appearances of truth from good, and garments signify truths, and hence the clothing of the understanding.

They have also similar houses, in which are apartments and chambers with courts as in the world, and within there are tables, benches, utensils, and various decorations. In heaven there are palaces so magnificent that palaces in the world cannot be compared to them. These palaces are of a magnitude so great, and of such symmetrical and architectural beauty, both without and within, and are decorated in such forms with gold and precious stones, that no picture painter on earth could possibly express them. There are also marble houses and houses of a blue color. The use of every apartment is known from its decorations.

They have also similar food and drink as in the world, and various kinds of food and drink are named.

In the spiritual world are likewise earths, mountains, hills, plains, grassy fields, paradises or gardens, groves and woods. There are ways everywhere tending to various societies, some are guarded. These ways then first appear to a spirit when he goes into his own society. There are also in that world fountains, lakes, and seas.

There appear likewise animals of the earth and all kinds of flying things, greater and smaller. There also appear compound animals, such as are described in the Word, there are also various insects or worms.

In a word, in the spiritual world there are not only similar things as in the natural world, but innumerable others; and everything exists with infinite variety and harmony, from which there breathes forth delight. In a word, in heaven there is a heaven in all and in each thing, in general and in every particular. Thus every external sense has its own heaven, and everything of the internal sense has also its own heaven, and an angel is a heaven in its least form, and each one, as he has heaven in himself, has also heaven outside of himself.

But it must be known that all things, and each now mentioned, are not material but spiritual, or are from a spiritual origin; and yet spirits know no otherwise than that they are material; the reason is, that when what is spiritual touches or tastes what is spiritual, it is altogether like when what is material touches or tastes what is material. Concerning this appearance I have often had a discussion with spirits, who believe that the things which they see and touch are material. I have shown them by various methods, and by various reasons even to the life, that nothing in the spiritual world is material, but that everything there is spiritual. I demonstrated it to them by the houses, which in a moment are formed, and in a moment are destroyed and dissipated; also by their garments, which in a moment are put on, and in a moment are changed; new garments are also given in a moment. In like manner I have demonstrated it from their dinners and repasts, showing that the tables upon which is the food, exist in a moment, and are afterwards dissipated in a moment; and that the spirits themselves can enter into the houses through the walls, and oftentimes not entering in through the doors. There was a certain individual known to me, with whom I conversed when his body which he had in the world was being buried, and I told him that he was now being buried, when he replied that he did not know what of him was being buried, because he had all things with him, a similar body as before, and other things similar, for he, like others, did not know otherwise than that he was still material, whereas he was spiritual. He was soon instructed that his material body, which he carried about with him in the world, and which then clothed his spiritual body, was being buried.

WONDERFUL THINGS [CONCERNING THE LANGUAGE OF SPIRITS]. Spirits and angels do not know otherwise than that they speak the same language they did in the world, write as they did in the world, and think as they did in the world, when yet they speak the spiritual language, in which there is no expression similar to any in the world; and they write by letters and characters; but it differs so much from writings in the world, that there is nothing whatever that is similar, except the letters and some points. Yea, they think altogether otherwise than in the world, so differently, that no thought is similar; but still they do not know otherwise than that all things are similar. That it is so I have often experienced by this, that spirits and angels when they are with me, are in my natural state; and it was said to them that in their spiritual state they should speak words and sentences, and retain the words with me in the natural state; and then there was not a single word alike, nor did they understand one of their words. They like-wise wrote a sentence in the spiritual state, and when it had been written it was shown in the natural state; there was nothing similar but the letters and points. Likewise when they thought in the spiritual state, they could not bring forth any idea of thought in the natural state. As for example, they say Rocky and to wish life [vitam velle]. Scopulosum in the spiritual language signifies that he casts out of doors, and vitam velle, that it is afar off. When they retain these expressions in the natural state, they do not understand them, nor any expression in the natural state when they come into the spiritual state. When they write scopulosum, they write —-, and when they write vitam velle, they write —-, and they suppose that they have written it fully. They write the sense of the words by alphabetic letters, each one of which signifies a thing —-. They write also by many signs, so that the greater the angelic wisdom is, the more things of wisdom they understand in the writing; the Word is thus written.

From these things it may be concluded that there is no ratio given by continuity between the natural and the spiritual; and that spirits and angels who are with men do not know that they are with them, nor an angel or a spirit that he is with a man. These wonderful things were disclosed to me before those in the spiritual world who were with me today, because they could be with me in my natural state and not before.

It is altogether similar between the thought, speech and writing of the angels of the Lord's celestial kingdom and of the angels of the spiritual kingdom, as there is between those who are in the spiritual kingdom in relation to those who are in the natural kingdom. This also has been confirmed by experience. 334-1

THE ENGLISH. The garments of the English are not like their garments in the world, neither those of the virgins nor of the women. They are adapted altogether to their general affection. When viewed in the spiritual state they appear graceful and beautiful, because they are altogether in agreement with their genius. But when the same are seen in their natural state, they do not appear so beautiful. The reason is that garments signify truths, and therefore all are clothed according to the reception of truth.

In London there are ten moderators of similar authority.

The understanding teaches the will and does not lead it, or faith teaches, but does not produce good works. For man can discern and see what is good and evil, but still act contrary there to, and then he either shuns it, or holds it in hatred, the will in the understanding is then opposite, yea in time dissipates it. Truth seen is what one acknowledges, but this is not the truth of life. But what once becomes of the will is either evil or good, this is stirred up by the sight and by the understanding, or the thought, and then the will is stirred up, and thence it exists in the thought. It is thus effected in all things reborn. It then appears as if the will was aroused by the thought; but it is not so. It is as if the sight should teach the feet to walk cautiously, and the hands to do the work. It appears as if that leads, but it does not lead, but shows and teaches. It is altogether like the heart and the lungs. The lungs do not respire unless the heart also acts, nor can there be given a reciprocal conjunction from the lungs but from the heart. See more below.

It is to be observed, that there may be anything either spiritual, moral or civil whose effect man has produced and thence has loved; the man hears it from another, or he reads it in a book. Thence it becomes his thought. In the thought there is raised up a perception of it, because this was the first of that thing. His affection is in the perception, thus the affection of truth. This affection which is called the affection of truth is from the affection of good, which is of the will, thus from the will in the affection of truth there is effected the conjunction of good and truth, in which conjunction the will and the understanding or good and truth act as one. Thus one is concealed in the other, within, and all are aroused from the ultimate, even through the hearing and sight, that is, the rousing up, namely because the will is concealed inmostly in the hearing, and thence in the thought, and it goes forth not otherwise than the spiritual sense and the celestial sense from the natural sense into the hearing, and thence sight is simultaneous. But it does not produce; production is effected by the will or the affection of good into the affection of truth, thence into the perception and from this into the thought; but not vice versa. From these things it is evident whence are appearances.

Thought is also given from hearing, and within the thought is perception, and within the perception is the affection of truth, and not at the same time the affection of the good of that truth. The affection of its good can be given with the love of self, of reputation, honor, and gain, but this is not marriage, but adultery. The reason is that this good which is merely natural, can be opposite to the good of truth itself, which is spiritual in various ways and respects. Examples may teach this.

When man is in his natural good, which in itself is evil, he then either does not know that [spiritual good], or denies it. He does so when he is in his proprium.

There is given the affection of knowing and understanding truth on account of glory, gain, and remuneration. The love of knowing and understanding is the love of natural light; the love of knowing and understanding truths is the love of spiritual light, which love is especially given with those who are in the love of good, but it is also given with those who are in the love of glory. From experience it has been given me to know that the love of light on account of glory as also of use is given with those who are in the love of evil; but with them the love of evil is then hidden or is lulled to sleep. It touches only the surface, as beauty from various colors, and the more it is hidden or lulled to sleep, the more it can feel delight. The love of knowing and understanding truths is from the external, which can be given provided the internal is hidden or is lulled to sleep; but it is a spurious love; it is like some filthy object covered over with a beautiful color, yea, with gold, underneath which surface there is evil. Therefore when good is in evil, one cannot know and understand those things, yea, he holds them in hatred, for he then confirms himself against truths. Thus the internal dissipates the external. Yea, there is given a holy external and a profane internal, the internal is lulled to sleep, but not the external; the external is not asleep.

IN THE TREATISE ON THE TEN COMMANDMENTS. It must treat of faith and of the understanding of truth.

What faith is. That there is conjunction with good works, and there is so much of faith as there is of life. That life is the soul of faith. That faith separate is not faith, it is inanimate. It is the dragon; it is the he-goat; it is Philistia; it is Cain; it is Reuben. What is faith? It is truth. At this day how sterile [is faith separate], and religion is nothing.

In heaven they altogether reject the dogma that the understanding is to be held under obedience to faith. All things of theology can be comprehended by the understanding. Not only by the spiritual understanding by the angels, but by the rational understanding by men. Otherwise from theological authority they could say whatever they wished.

FOODS. There were some in the lowest heaven, to whom the atmosphere above appeared like water. I spoke with them and they said that they have choice foods, and they take them from the table and keep them until evening, and eat therefrom at will; but it is not allowed them to hide them until morning. This is what is meant in the Lord's prayer, "Give us daily bread." Concerning the manna it is said that it bred worms when it was kept. Then they were to burn up what was left of the paschal lamb; neither should they let anything from the sacrifices remain over; also that the bread of faces should be replaced anew every day. Thence it is evident why everyone is provided with spiritual daily bread by the Lord, and that it is not given as their own, and thus there should be no care concerning tomorrow, what they should eat and drink. Thus and not otherwise are good spirits in their works, and in their life and faith. Nothing is given to the evil, but only to him who is in work. Thus also all are held in bonds, thus every use is remunerated. [Marginal Note:] Some are nourished at the tables of others, but those who are evil and hateful sit at the table and do not see the food.

MARRIAGE AND ADULTERY. Adultery is hell itself, thus it is the Devil himself and Satan. It has been shown by many things as also by experience, that all in hell are adulterers, that they rage like furies when they perceive conjugial love; which is a sign that they are from hell; that they desire to violate chaste marriages, and many other things; then that they are in the marriage of evil and falsity. Marriage is heaven itself because all there are in conjugial love, everyone in his own degree. That love is the fundamental love of all the loves of heaven, because an angel by it becomes love in form, because they who are in marriage are in good and truth; and therefore heaven cooperates in marriages and nuptials and hell in adulteries and whoredoms. Thence it follows that as far as a man detests adulteries as a diabolic sin, and looks to the Lord, so far he is in a like degree in heaven.

Marriage and adultery must be treated of especially, because he who is in marriage is in the conjunction of good and truth but he who is in adultery is in evil and falsity. And because adultery is all sin against the Decalogue, for he who is in that is in all the evil of the Decalogue and vice versa; and because these are involved and as it were contained in marriage and adultery in summaries, therefore they must be treated of especially. At this day in the Christian world adulteries are more prevalent than in any other religion, because they separate good from truth or charity from faith; and when these are separated, then from influx it cannot be otherwise. Therefore they confirm adulteries and not marriages; and therefore it is not known what conjugial love is, it must be shown how the faith of the present day separates and thus falsifies the Word, then how it perverts man's rational, thence adulteries are delightful, but not so marriages.

Adulteries are the worst of all abominations, because the seed of man is his life which is conjoined with the life of the wife, so that they are not two but one flesh; but when the lives of many men are immitted into one woman, there becomes such foulness that on account of the abomination it cannot be described, it becomes such before the angels. 348-1

TO DO GOODS AND NOT TO FIGHT AGAINST EVILS IS TO DO GOODS FROM SELF AND NOT FROM THE LORD. It is believed by many that they will be saved because they have done goods, as that they have given to the poor, benefitted their neighbor, acted sincerely and justly in their duty and work, and yet have never fought against the evils opposed to their goods; believing that thus evils are removed. It appears to them, moreover, as if goods removed evils; saying in heart, "If I do good then I shall avoid evil." Nevertheless the case is as follows: that such a one does good from obedience to the precepts of the Lord, yet not from the Lord but from himself, thus not from any spiritual law except only apparently, but from a moral and civil law actually. In this case his evils nevertheless remain; for although he does not do them, yet he is not averse to them. Consequently when the love of evil with its delight returns, he does not resist the evil, but either excuses it and does it, or omits doing it on account of himself and the world; moreover, he does not then know that it is evil. The case is otherwise when he fights against evil from the spiritual law; for, insofar as he does this, he censures evil, and he then loves good and its truth; and in proportion as he does good from the Lord and not from himself, in the same proportion the Lord, by the good and truth in the man, removes his evils.

I have heard spirits saying, that they know no otherwise than that to do good is to shun evil. But they receive for reply, that in this case they no otherwise shun evil than that they do not do it; but that nevertheless they do not hold evil in hatred, and reject it as sin, unless as far as they have fought against it. By fighting against it evil is removed, and then good succeeds, that is, by combat the devil is removed and the Lord enters. To do good, and not to fight against evil, is to do good only in externals and not in internals; but to fight against evil and thus to do good, is to do good in internals. Man is not made spiritual except by combat. Some of those who have been sincere, just, chaste, and have not fought against what is insincere, unjust, and unchaste, are after death let into combats, and then it clearly appears how much they have done good from themselves, or on account of themselves, or from the Lord; and by combats they are reformed.

Footnotes

334-1 Following n. in Tafel's Latin text is a paragraph "On the Spiritual Sense;" this and numbers following 339, 347, and 355 properly belong to The Word of the Lord from Experience, where they will be found in this volume. Nos. xxi., xxii., xxiii., xxiv. and xxvi. We make our numbering of paragraphs consecutive.

336-1 Following n. 328 in Tafel's Latin text is a paragraph "On the Spiritual Sense;" this and numbers following 339, 347, and 355 properly belong to The Word of the Lord from Experience, where they will be found in this volume. Nos. xxi., xxii., xxiii., xxiv. and xxvi. We make our numbering of paragraphs consecutive.

348-1 Following n. 326 in Tafel's Latin text is a paragraph "On the Spiritual Sense;" this and numbers following 339, 347, and 355 properly belong to The Word of the Lord from Experience, where they will be found in this volume. Nos. xxi., xxii., xxiii., xxiv. and xxvi. We make our numbering of paragraphs consecutive.

Before this they do not come into the affection of truth; nor their hearts into the perception and knowledge of it; nor are they taught what evil is and what good is. Their former state is thus one of ignorance.

Man does good from obedience, and he does good also from affection. He does good from obedience before he has fought against evil. This is the first state of man, and it may be a state of reformation; and he who is in this state and does not do evils is regenerated in the other life by combats against them or by temptations. To do good from affection takes place only when man has fought against evils; this is the state of man's regeneration and this state is the inverse of the former.

To do good from obedience is not from freedom, because not from affection; in it there is the thought of reward, and consequently afterwards of merit. In proportion as man shuns evils as sins, in the same proportion he does good not from himself but from the Lord. In proportion as man shuns evil, in the same proportion his works become works of charity.

No one can do good from himself; it is the Lord with man who does the good, and no one comes to the Lord but he who removes evils from himself by combats against them. Hence it is that in proportion as anyone thus removes evils, in the same proportion he does good from the Lord; and this good appears in like manner as if it were done by the man, but nevertheless the man always thinks of the Lord, and the angels have a perception that is from the Lord.

THE DELIGHT FROM THE GLORY OF BEING WISE, AND THE DELIGHT OF COMMANDING. The delight from the glory of being wise, and the delight of commanding I have sometimes seen that when they were in the delight of the love of ruling, they acted like foolish persons, believing then that they were wiser than others. But when they were turned about they were led back into their understanding. They then saw that they had been foolish. But because they more greatly loved that former delight which was foolish, and turned themselves continually to that foolishness, they then seemed to be in that wisdom, thus by turns, and still their understanding could not lead them back, but the will led. Concerning this many may be named from experience, as Charles XII., Benz, and others. This is a manifest sign that the will acts into the understanding, and not the understanding into the will. Nor is it so that they are converted by the Lord in the understanding by an influx of light into the voluntary, and that they are converted by hell to the delight of the will.

THE TEN COMMANDMENTS. The Ten Commandments As far as man fights against evils as sins, and shuns evils as sins, so far the works which he does are goods, and so far they are charity.

As far as a man shuns evils as sins so far his spiritual mind is opened. -So far his life becomes spiritual moral. -So far he is in heaven, thus in the Lord, and the Lord is in him. -So far he comes into the light of heaven, thus into the affection of truth on account of the truth. -So far he is being regenerated, and is regenerated. -So far the order is inverted and he acts from the will of good, and as if from the understanding. -So far he is purified by truths. -So far hereditary evil is removed. -So far he increases in intelligence and wisdom. -Many similar things from the heavenly doctrine where it treats of what is meant by truths. -This is done successively, and afterward to eternity. -So far he has faith.

THE MORAVIANS. They said that they were the remains of the Apostolic Church, and therefore they call each other brothers. Therefore some from their society who were below the earth, were sent to those who had been converted in the time of Paul and the Apostles and were of the church.

First they came to the church which was with the Collossian nations, and they spoke with them at first as if they were of such a church, but they were questioned concerning the Lord; they said that they pray to the Father for the sake of the Son, and that they do not go to the Son. They answered that they go to the Lord, because He said that He is the way, the truth and the life; and that no one cometh to the Father except through Him: then that one must have faith in Him, and that they cannot go to the Father immediately, thus it is that they ascend above what is permitted. They were questioned about charity. They said that they have charity among themselves, and therefore they call each other brethren; but they said that this is friendship and not charity, and they asked whether they do not know that charity is to do good, and that this is primary, and that they should call good brother, and truth companion. But when they said that to do good effects nothing for salvation, thus charity effects nothing, but faith alone, and that faith is that the Lord was sent by the Father that He might take away the damnation of the law by the passion of the cross, it was seen that they are no longer under any law, then being indignant they drove them away, calling them fanatics and not Apostolical.

They who were of the Thessalonian church said the same of them. But these only inspected them from above and they recognized similar things with them, and being indignant they turned themselves away, as from those who are to be altogether guarded against.

Afterwards they came to a certain Apostolic church, which was in Galilee not far from Tyre. There they did the same, asserting that they were in a like doctrine with them. But they were questioned concerning the Word, they said that they had the Epistles of Paul, in which is their doctrine itself, and that he spoke from the Holy Spirit. They were asked what they believe concerning the Gospels, they answered that the Lord there spoke from Himself. They were asked whether He spoke from the Father, thus from the Divine or from the Holy Spirit. They said that He spoke from Himself. They asked how; [they replied] simply as a man, and that He did not speak from the Father nor from the Divine, because He wished them to have faith in Him, and wished to be equal to the Father. They asked whether He was conceived from the Father; they said that they would think of this as they wished, they did not dare to say that [they thought] as the Jews did, nor did they dare to say that they hold in low estimation what He spoke. They were questioned about the Old Testament, whether it is holy, they said that the Jews regard it as holy because [it was given] through them; but that they do not regard it as holy, and that it is evil to believe that it is holy by itself. They were asked whether they know that there are many things therein concerning the Coming of the Lord; they said that it is about the Coming of the Messiah, and that by the Messiah is meant God the Father and not the Lord, denying that the Father was in the Lord, according to His Word. When passages were quoted therefrom concerning the Lord, they turned themselves away and said that they understand it differently from them. In a word they reject the Word of the Old Testament as not holy, and as having nothing there concerning the Lord. Some things which they answered, because they hurt the ears, I pass by. Afterward they heard concerning their faith, and they said that it does not at all agree with their faith and that it is nothing, and being indignant that they had said they were of their church, they commanded them to depart, and otherwise they would drive them away, because they see that they are not Christians at all, calling them antichrists.

Zinzendorf heard all those things which they spoke with this and the former Apostolic church, and he grieved, saying, "I know not whence such things have come to pass since I was in the world;" and seeing that there was nothing for them but hell, he grieved. They said they would not turn to them, because they would thus disturb them, and misfortunes would happen to them.

They said they take something from the Gospels, the prophecies and the histories of the Old Testament in their preaching; chiefly things which confirm their dogmas; something also on account of the rest of Christians, lest they should give offense, and that they may allure to their side.

It was asked whence they could become such in the world, when yet they pray to the Father, and are religious. Answer was made them, because they deny the Divine of the Lord. And they were instructed that there is a general efflux from hell against the Divine of the Lord, against charity towards the neighbor, and against the holiness of the Word, and that they may know from this whence they have the confirmations against those three things.

Some hundreds of them came out and went to a society where charity reigns, and they were in the persuasion that they were living and those who were in charity were dead. From that persuasion the angels of the society of charity appeared before their eyes as blackish, and they themselves in some degree exteriorly as angels. Their persuasion has this in it, that as they draw near they appear to themselves from their persuasion as if they were living, and the rest before their eyes as if half dead. When they perceive this, they pray to the Lord that the newcomers be removed from them, therefore those over them are commanded to go away; but as they depart and are at a distance, they appear monstrous, so that they are scarcely men, and that monstrous appearance increases even until their entrance under the earth, which was a cavern; and when they come thither the monstrosity remains and appears before their eyes and the eyes of their brethren; and afterwards for a long time they are punished many times, nor do they approach anymore to other societies and by persuasion induce others to such things, and thus allure them to their insane dogma, and believe that they are living; and those who are in charity are unwilling to be continually with them. The punishment continues until they affirm that they will no longer do thus; for their greatest desire is to allure and lead over to their side by various cunning ways and arts; they are deceivers.

FAITH. 366-1 The Lord from eternity, who is Jehovah, came into the world that He might effect the Last Judgment and at the same time glorify His Human, and without this no mortal could have been saved; and they are saved who believe in Him and do good from Him. This is the faith of the New Jerusalem.

As far as faith is separated from the goods of charity it differs from that faith. Let him explore it who is able. Faith separate supposes: That God the

Father and God the Son are two, both from eternity. It supposes that God the Son came into the world from the will of God the Father that He might make satisfaction for the human race, otherwise from the Divine justice, which they also call vindictive, it would have perished in eternal death. It supposes that satisfaction was made by the Lord's fulfilling the law and by the passion of the cross. It supposes that the mercy of God the Father was on account of those things of the Son. It supposes imputation, the ascription of His merit to them who are in that faith, and who from it pray to the Father to have mercy for the Son's sake. It supposes the justification of those who thus pray from trust and confidence. It supposes the operation of the Holy Spirit with them. It supposes the remission of all sins with them and thus salvation. It supposes that then they will have an endeavor to do good, which deeply hidden operates, but not manifestly, and moves the will of man. Others, whom they believe to be less learned, suppose a manifest operation. But most of those who confirm themselves in that faith, suppose that no one can do good from himself which is good, unless it is meritorious, thence that no good work saves, but faith alone; they say nothing about evil and about good of life, nor do they think of it. Some suppose that the influx of faith is instantaneous, and also that it is given in the last hour of death, and that their salvation is by faith alone howsoever they have lived. [Marginal Note:] They suppose there is something of temptation, and that liberation is by that faith.

In a summary, that God the Father sent the Son to make satisfaction for the human race, and that they who believe in Him are saved from His merit.

They divide into parties concerning instantaneous salvation by faith and vindictive justice.

Their books are full of these things, but they write confirmations of these subjects only.

Faith places the understanding under obedience to this faith, and he does not understand what the truth of faith is.

THE MORAVIANS. I spoke with them of their brotherhood, whether it is of love or charity, they said no, but only of friendship, because they are of one opinion; they do not admit the expression love and charity in religion. Argument Concerning the Judgment By the judgments which have preceded, preparation has been made for the universal judgment. Concerning the new heavens which they made for themselves. Concerning the going forth of some before the Last Judgment, who were in faith separate. And that they were first visited and separated. Who they were that made for themselves heavens]. It was seen that they acted there as in Sodom. There were seen rocks carried away like a cloud. Those who were in faith alone betook themselves upon rocks. How they dwelt there. Earthquakes preceded. The wicked spirits in the plain were cast out. And the good reserved by the Lord were taken up in their place, and this is to open the sepulchers The destructions which preceded the Last Judgment. How the Divine sphere enters into them and thence opens up their interiors. The quality of those upon whom the Last Judgment was effected. The arrangement of the Reformed before the judgment, also where and how they were arranged. How they were first led forth. The casting down of those in faith alone. And then exploration. Likewise others. Likewise others. Likewise others. How they were then seen]. Their dispersion. The angels wondered at such faith. They have no conscience. The purifying of the middle lasts a long time. Some were seen at a table, clothed as with wedding garments, but within they were robbers. They were cast down. They appeared as if sincere, yet they are wolves within. Their lot. The exploration of the Reformed as to their quality, and their distinction into classes. Their ideas of the Lord. Of those who were in piety and external worship. Their lot. Hypocrites, their lot. Priests who read the Word only that they may preach it. Their lot. They are separated according to the internals of life which are affections. Dragons, how they are explored. Who those are who are in confirmation and in pride. What they are. What is draconic. Anyone can know what charity is, that it is not to steal, etc.. The good who were left were allotted their habitations. Those who have understood and known many things, and with whom there was no will of good. Their lot. Those who have not acknowledged the Lord, and have no good of charity; their rebellion and conjunction with the papists and Mohammedans. Something said of the combat of the dragon with Michael. The Lord seen in a cloud. A representation of a tail. Those who are in faith alone and in the love of commanding look downward. How they are distinguished according to their idea of God. Five classes. They persecuted me by inspirations and at the same time respirations and pulse; experience thence. The thought of those who are in faith alone described. Their quality was such although they had not thought wickedly. Such were let out of the hells, they believing that they would then act well, but in vain, they were in anguish. The arrangement into societies. The purification of societies. The arrangement takes place according to the affections of the life. Not according to the affections of the understanding. The nature of their ways afterwards. The most perfect arrangement is that of the Reformed. The reason is that they have the Word and they go to the Lord. How they are taken up into heaven. The Word of the Lord, they who have faith as a seed of mustard. The goats and their combats. In like manner ,the dragon. Why it treats of them in Revelation. Draconic spirits. The power of truth in the spiritual world. Those who have little of life, how life is inspired into them. The religion of those who are in faith alone, it is only knowledge. They who combat against evils receive the law as if inscribed on themselves. Conducted into a mansion of heaven. What is the opinion in the third heaven concerning those in faith alone; it is only knowledge. According as they lived in the world so is their heaven. The quality of those who are in faith alone, and its quality as it interiorly appears. How the Epistle of James appears to them. They are received who believe in charity, provided they have lived the life of charity. One was turned about but he turned back afterwards. The arrangement of those who are in the faith of charity. In their factitious heavens there was a wintry light. The hells where they continually wrangle about their faith. Their quality. By experience those who believed that they had faith, it was given them to know that they had no faith. Their interiors were closed. They had a religion of the memory. They were sensual. Faith alone of the church is not given, from experience. Those who are in no affection of truth, and yet reason much about truths, experience. Those who are in faith alone have no conscience. Those who believe in charity and do not live the life of charity, are not much unlike [those in faith alone]. How faith separate leads to evil of life. I spoke with Melancthon about faith alone, how false it is. Those who are in faith alone cannot be saved, what their quality is. Because all the societies of heaven are arranged according to the differences of love. An Englishman who wished to conjoin charity with faith, but it was not recognized. I read before the English their prayer before the Eucharist, and my discourse with them. English presbyters who made an idol of their faith. Discourse with the English concerning faith alone. The nature of their arguments for faith alone. Those were explored who confessed faith in the last hour of death; their quality. After the judgment many of those from faith alone were collected and rejected. Afterwards many wished to receive charity, but in vain, the reason. The endeavor after justification. Free will with them. It is not allowed them to preach; the hearers go out. The deserts where those are who are in faith alone. They were explored whether they know anything true and it was found that they do not. Conversation with angels concerning the progression of truth to good. How the English write their discourses. That faith saves no one, a few things. It is like a dark chamber]. Their miserable state who have regarded evils as allowable, and their internal. All the states of love return after death, thus the states of faith if it enters the love. At this day they crucify the Lord. The ideas at this day concerning God, heaven, love, faith. The first state of man after death. Love produces the knowledge of every good in the thought. They who are in the love of self cannot be admitted into heaven. They who are in the love of self can equally speak of the Divine, but yet after death they are against the Divine. They are enemies of the Lord]. Two opposite dominions of love. Their interiors and quality. Examples from those in the equestrian order. Love corresponds to flame, faith to light. The quality of those who worship the Lord from spiritual love. Affection makes the man, from changes induced and correspondences. The delight of the love of commanding exceeds every other delight. The delight of the love of commanding, into what it is turned after death. Everyone after death comes into his own love. Fr. Gyll, his mode of praying. The quality after death of him who is in the delight of commanding. Dreadful example [of hatred] against the Lord with those who think nothing from religion in their life.

Footnotes
366-1 Following n. 326 in Tafel's Latin text is a paragraph "On the Spiritual Sense;" this and numbers following 339, 347, and 355 properly belong to The Word of the Lord from Experience, where they will be found in this volume. Nos. xxi., xxii., xxiii., xxiv. and xxvi. We make our numbering of paragraphs consecutive.